THE ALLURE OF
DEEP WOODS

BACKPACKING THE NORTHVILLE-PLACID TRAIL

by Walt McLaughlin

NORTH COUNTRY BOOKS, INC.
Utica, New York

ISBN-10 1-59531-043-6
ISBN-13 978-1-59531-043-9

Design by Zach Steffen & Rob Igoe, Jr.

Library of Congress Cataloging-in-Publication Data

McLaughlin, Walt.
  The allure of deep woods : backpacking the Northville-Placid trail / by Walt McLaughlin.
    pages cm
  ISBN 978-1-59531-043-9 (alk. paper)
  1.   Backpacking--New York (State)--Northville-Lake Placid Trail--Guidebooks. 2.
Northville-Lake Placid Trail (N. Y.)--Guidebooks. I. Title.
  GV199.42.N652N675 2013
  796.5109747--dc23
                        2013010664

North Country Books, Inc.
220 Lafayette Street
Utica, New York 13502
www.northcountrybooks.com

Acknowledgments

HIKING THE NORTHVILLE-PLACID TRAIL wouldn't even be possible if it weren't for the tireless efforts of the folks at the New York State Department of Environmental Conservation. Many thanks to them and the Adirondack Mountain Club volunteers who help them maintain the trail. Thanks also to Limps-a-Little, Bob and Lynn, Bruce and Marty, and the others I met along the way for infusing an otherwise solitary journey with much-needed warmth and humanity.

Rob Igoe, Jr., the president of North Country Books, has kept faith in this book despite recent upheavals in the publishing industry. Zach Steffen, the company's general manager, has worked hard ushering it into print. I am fortunate to have both of these men in my camp, along with everyone else at NCB.

Then there is my wife, Judy, who urges me to take a hike whenever I grow restless, and tolerates all my moods and idiosyncrasies while I'm writing about it afterward. I'd be lost without her.

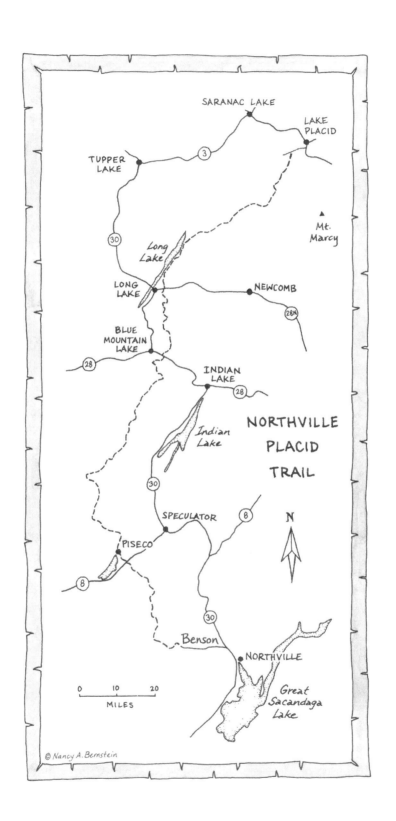

Chapter 1

"YOU'RE GOING TO GET WET," Judy says as raindrops collect on the windshield. I nod my head in agreement, flipping on the wipers one more time. A thin drizzle started several hours ago, shortly after we ramped onto I-87 and headed south into the Adirondacks. It's been raining off and on ever since, but that's really beside the point. Like most curt exchanges between two people who have been married as long as we have, more is being said here than words indicate. Inclement weather won't be the only hardship. There will be plenty of sweat, stiff joints, and aching muscles, and a boggy trail, as well. More importantly, we will be apart for two weeks. When Judy finally voices our mutual apprehension about this, I shrug my shoulders, saying that that's just the price one has to pay for a good dose of deep woods solitude. She's well aware of this and is willing to accept her portion of the bill on my behalf. Two weeks goes by fast at our age, I assure her. Judy changes the subject.

The early September rain ends just before we reach the trailhead half a mile west of Upper Benson. I write my name in the trailhead register, formally announcing to the world that I intend to hike all 122 miles of the long, winding, backcountry trail from here to Lake Placid. Judy wants a picture for posterity, so I stand next to a big sign marking the southernmost end of the Northville-Placid Trail. I feel absurd. I swore off long-distance hiking years ago, after concluding that nonstop movement isn't the best way to appreciate wild nature. Yet here I am, ready to do it all over again—different time and place, but the same urge to make tracks. Judy snaps the photo while a day hiker from New Jersey signs into the nearby register. His sudden appearance adds one more layer of absurdity to the moment. He hovers in the background, trying to figure out where to park his car while Judy and I kiss goodbye. I say something stupid like "See you in two weeks" before walking down the dirt road, towards the actual beginning of the trail. When I look back, Judy is gone.

After a couple hundred yards of graded gravel and dirt, the road morphs into a pair of rutted tracks. I enter the woods, skirting rather large mud puddles in the middle of the trail. I run a gauntlet of "No Trespassing" signs before the first blue trail marker appears. These unwelcoming notices continue until I reach the Adirondack Forest Preserve. A bright yellow and blue sign marks the Preserve boundary. I drop my pack and stretch my legs.

The New Jersey day hiker and his dog come along while I'm stretching. He stops to chat briefly. He isn't carrying as much as a butt-pack, so he skips away quickly once the obligatory pleasantries have been exchanged. I shoulder my heavy pack a few minutes later, huffing and puffing down the trail after him.

The tracks split into two narrow trails at a small, nondescript clearing. The Northville-Placid Trail turns sharply to the left, following a clear, rocky stream. Now it's a well-marked footpath winding through the trees, and I'm one happy hiker. I meander nice and cool through a mix of hardwoods and conifers. The soft earth is easy on the feet. The steady rush of nearby water—the North Branch of West Stony Creek—is a soothing soundtrack. According to my map, I'm entering the Silver Lake Wilderness Area. It stretches northward twenty miles or so, all the way to the town of Piseco. That puts a smile on my face. I'm in my element, at long last.

I cross a rather elaborate wooden bridge spanning the animated stream. I'm so impressed by this structure that I stop and take a picture of it. If this bridge is any indication of how well maintained the N-P Trail is, then my trek will be an easy one. I drop my pack, dig out a disposable camera and snap away. Then, with my backpack already on the ground, I take a long, unnecessary break. I sit next to the stream, admiring it while downing half a liter of water and a couple handfuls of trail mix. A stream this clear always comes as something of a surprise when I've been away from the woods for a while. I lose myself in its transparent pools, white riffles, and swirling eddies.

The day hiker and his dog suddenly appear, bounding down the trail. I stand up, saying "hi" and "goodbye" as they shoot past. They're on their way out. Good. Now I have this forest all to myself.

IN THE TOP, FRONT PANTS POCKET on my right thigh, I keep a carefully folded topographical map in a clear plastic bag. The Adirondack Mountain Club created this map for people like me—people looking to hike the Northville-Placid Trail end-to-end. Along with a little advice about what to do if you get lost or injured, there are hiking and camping guidelines in the upper right corner of the map. "Do not hike alone," is number one on that list. It's the only guideline that I blatantly and repeatedly ignore. The others I practice religiously. They are all common backcountry practices intended to either preserve the wild or safeguard those traveling through it. Guidelines like "don't use soap in a brook" and "carry a compass and know how to use it" make perfect sense to me. I preach them to others, in fact. Considering how big and wild the Adirondacks are, "do not hike alone" is probably the most important guideline of them all. But I can't abide by it.

Wilderness is, by definition, an unforgiving place. A hiker traveling alone though wild country is much like an acrobat doing aerial stunts without a net. No, I don't recommend it. Yet I hike by myself on a regular basis because deep woods solitude does something to me that nothing else can. Alone in the wild, my head clears. Alone in the wild, the world seems all right and the meaninglessness that nips at my heels back in the lowlands fades away. As much as I love crystal-clear water, green forests, and animal encounters, solitude is the main reason I keep coming out here. Time and again, I find myself turning to the wild as if my life depends on it. I drink the wild like a tonic, certain that without a regular dose of it, I'd shrivel up and blow away.

If hiking alone isn't prudent, then hiking alone when you're my age is downright foolish. Oddly enough, age is the other big reason I'm taking on a hundred-plus miles of rough, wild country. This trek is a belated birthday present to myself. Last spring, I turned fifty. That was a watershed of sorts. My father had his first heart operation right after he turned fifty. I've known several fifty-year-olds who have died. I'm a firm believer that, when it comes to the body, you either use it or lose it. If I don't keep moving, I'll turn into a blob, thus making premature death more likely. Backcountry trekking is the only form of rigorous exercise that I really enjoy.

I hiked Vermont's 270-mile Long Trail end-to-end in the mid-1990s. It wasn't easy then. How much more difficult would it be today? Hard to say. All I know is that I'm softer, heavier, and much less flexible than I was a decade ago. I spend way too much time in front of a computer screen, plopped in a chair like a sack of potatoes. So what's the main cause of my steadily eroding physical condition then, age or disuse? What difference does that make? Either way, I have to get back on the move again.

Six months ago, I started training for this trip, and I've hiked three or four times a week since then. I reduced my food intake in order to shed a few pounds. Stretching has become part of my regular routine, as well. Five days ago, I went to my doctor for a physical and received a clean bill of health. My body is as ready for a trip like this as it will ever be. So here I am, on the trail with a fifty-five-pound pack on my back, good boots on my feet, and trekking poles in hand, giving it my best shot.

Although I hate to admit it, I want the brag of having hiked this trail at one throw. Unlike my stint on the Long Trail, when I really didn't care whether I finished or not, I want to do it all this time. I want to prove to myself that I can still do it. I want to stop the steady erosion of my physical options. I'm not ready to retire my expedition backpack, thus settling for day hikes or overnighters. Not just yet.

THE GROUND AROUND ME becomes rougher and wilder as I hike steadily uphill, venturing deeper into the forest. The trail itself reflects this change, becoming muddier, narrower, more cluttered with roots and rocks. A thick mist hangs in the trees. My eyeglasses steam up. The air is so heavy with water right now that it could be raining. I can't tell whether it is or not. Suddenly a thin drizzle commences, thus resolving the matter. After crossing a small brook, I drop my pack and dig out a backpack cover. Good thing I do. By the time I have it draped over my pack, the drizzle has escalated to a steady shower. Should I put on raingear? No, I'd only sweat inside it. Better to stay cool, hiking in a wet t-shirt. So I put on a rain hat and leave it at that.

Rock Lake is barely visible through the trees. The rain nixes a side trip down to the lake for a better view. I plod along, planting my trekking poles in the slippery mud, sidestepping puddles whenever I can. Eventually I reach a rather large stream—the headwaters of the Sacandaga River's West Branch. I cross it, then turn sharply to the right. I follow this stream all the way to Meco Lake, passing several small waterfalls along the way. They cascade into foamy, dark amber pools with high-pitched roars, causing me to forget the weather for a while.

Meco Lake is a shallow body of water with marshy edges. Ideal moose habitat. I stop and look around but don't see any of those large, lumbering creatures. No matter. The cloud-grey light washing over the placid water is a welcome break from forest gloom. I soak it in during a short break, before resuming my walk along the lake's shoreline. Unfortunately, the trail underfoot is an ankle-twister, with lots of roots and mud holes, so I can't look around much once I'm moving again. At the northern end of the lake, the trail veers back into the dark forest. Not much to see in this misty, green-leaf infinity. Soaking wet and footsore, I tramp the last mile of today's seven-and-a-half mile hike without stopping.

When Silver Lake finally appears, I let out a sigh of relief. I spot the lean-to right after skirting the edge of the lake. It's a typical Adirondack-style lean-to: a modest, three-sided structure about seven feet deep and ten feet wide. With its sharply sloping roof and prominent overhang, the lean-to provides ample protection from the elements. Even though the steady rain has tapered again to a mere drizzle, I'm quite pleased to have reached this shelter. It's the only dry place for miles in any direction.

Immediately after dropping my pack, I strip off my wet t-shirt and don a dry one. I'll get out of my wet pants and boots later. First I have to sling a line into the trees for my food bags, fetch some water from the lake, and fix dinner. No campfire tonight. The forest is too wet and I'm too tired. Besides, it's getting late. There's not more than an hour of daylight left. I have to eat, clean up, and get the food bags off the ground before any bears come around. Can't afford to lose any provisions this early in the trip.

Down by the shoreline, a hundred feet or so from the lean-to, I gaze across the broad lake. I half expect to see something human. I crouch on rocks along the water's edge while refilling my water bottles, watching long, wispy strands of mist creep slowly past distant wooded hills. The silence is disarming. Water laps to shore—that is all. No songbirds, trout jumping, or glorious sunset. A great, wild silence. Only then does it occur to me where I am. It's difficult to grasp, really. I'm not completely here yet. I wait for lights to suddenly appear on the opposite shoreline despite the fact that there are no cabins over there. Is anyone else camped on this lake? No sign of them if they are. Apparently my only neighbors are wild animals.

A bit later, while settling into the lean-to for the night, I hear a great horned owl hooting in the distance. I hear another one shortly after turning off my headlamp and burrowing deep into my sleeping bag. Then fatigue sets in. Dueling owls call out in the middle of the night. I barely hear them in the netherworld between wakefulness and dreams. Then slowly I let go of that other life of mine beyond the forest. Even as some part of me resists it, I give myself over to the wild.

Chapter 2

THE HAUNTING CALL OF A LOON draws me from a deep slumber. I open my eyes to twilight, then roll back over for another hour. When finally I rise from bed, I take stock of my physical complaints. Actually, I feel pretty good—a little achy in the hips and shoulders but good overall. I drop my food bags to the ground and fix breakfast. A woodpecker knocks in the distance. Nuthatches creep up and down nearby trees. A chipmunk comes into camp while I'm eating. I toss a few nuts his way. Then a thrush lands on a low branch on the edge of camp, checking me out. Plenty of company this morning, but I'm alone all the same. I haven't seen one of my own kind since that New Jersey day hiker cleared out of the woods yesterday afternoon.

After the pot of water on my camp stove has boiled a minute or two, I make coffee. Forgot to pack filters, so the coffee grounds swirl about wildly in my cup when I pour water over them. "Hobo coffee" is what old timers call it. I let the grounds settle to the bottom before taking a sip. It's passable. This'll have to do until I reach Piseco. Hard to believe that I forgot to pack coffee filters. Oh well. No matter how well I prepare for an outing, I always forget something.

Bright red and orange maple leaves litter the otherwise barren ground around the fire pit. It's an undisputable sign of the season. Today is Labor Day—that place on the calendar sharply delineating summer from fall.

The autumnal equinox is still several weeks away, but children are going back to school now so everyone's thinking fall. Here at two thousand feet above sea level, the seasonal change is quite apparent already. Autumn gets a head start in the highlands. Many of the leaves overhead are turning color, and the air this morning has a slight chill to it. Who knows? I might even awaken to frost at some point during the next two weeks.

MIDMORNING ON THE TRAIL. Once I've hiked long enough to warm up my muscles, I stop to stretch. I do this per Michelle's instructions. Michelle is the massage therapist who kept my strained right shoulder from seizing up last year. For a while, I couldn't lift my arm above my chest. But a few months after Michelle got her hands on it, my shoulder became fully functional again. She refuses to take all the credit, though. Praise those skillful hands of hers and she'll insist that stretching on a regular basis is at least half of the healing process. When I asked her what I should do to prepare myself physically for this trip, she told me to stretch hips, legs, back, and shoulders. "Stretch every day," she said. So that's what I'm doing.

Ten minutes of stretching, then I'm back on the move. I follow two sets of tracks pressed deep into the mud. A man and his dog put those tracks there. Don't know the guy's name but his dog is called Pip. I remember that much from the trailhead register, where the man signed-in right before me. I call Pip's owner The Trekker because he wrote in the register that he intends to hike the entire Northville-Placid Trail in eight or nine days. Now that's what I call serious hiking. He started two days ahead of me so his tracks have eroded somewhat. But the rain hasn't washed them away where the trail is especially soft and muddy. I follow those tracks, wondering where everyone else went—all the hikers who didn't sign into the register. Surely The Trekker and I aren't the only ones out here.

The Trekker marched straight through mud holes, full speed ahead. Pip skirted the softer, wetter places, keeping to slightly higher ground. At first I step where The Trekker stepped, not wanting to widen the trail into a cattle path. I end up deferring to Pip's better judgment, though. Don't mind getting my boots muddy, but falling down is definitely something I want to avoid. Even with trekking poles to keep my balance, I've already slipped twice. So I follow Pip's tracks through the worst of it.

A mile north of Silver Lake, the terrain becomes exceptionally rough and wild. Plenty of downed trees crisscrossed every which way; plenty of undergrowth. A sea of hobblebush and striped maple, accompanied by ferns and club moss, spreads as far across the forest floor as I can see. Much of the hobblebush has turned deep reddish brown and some of the striped maples have yellowed in anticipation of autumn, thus making the forest understory quite beautiful to behold. That said, I'm fully aware that getting through this tangle would be nearly impossible without the trail. I pass through dozens of cuts in downed trees and climb over an uncut one every ten minutes or so. Thank God for trail clearing crews! Without them this path would have disappeared into the bush a long time ago.

I hear a tree come crashing down and then, a few minutes later, see a huge hemlock broken away from its roots and lying on top of saplings still covered with fresh green leaves. No doubt the folks at New York's Department of Environmental Conservation have their hands full trying to keep this trail open. Hikers often criticize the DEC for not doing a better job maintaining the trail, but that's only because they don't realize how much effort it takes. I went on a trail clearing outing through Vermont's Green Mountains once. It wasn't easy carrying a chainsaw over several miles of rough terrain. Can't imagine hauling one across country like this. Many of the downed trees here are big and old. Cutting through them would be no mean feat. Some are four feet thick. Yeah, this forest has been here a while.

WHEN THE ADIRONDACK MOUNTAIN CLUB was chartered in 1922, the unlikely brainchild of a developer named Meade Dodson and oil company officer George D. Pratt, the first order of business was to cut a trail the length of the Adirondacks. Originally known as the Long Trail, it later became the Northville-Placid Trail to avoid any confusion with the Long Trail being blazed in neighboring Vermont. By the end of 1923, the entire route was rough-cut. During the two years that followed, the Club greatly improved it. That's when people started hiking this trail. The Adirondack Forest Preserve, through which most of the trail passes, had been in existence for several decades by then.

The New York State Legislature created the Forest Preserve in the late 1800s in order to keep parts of the Catskills and Adirondacks "forever wild." When that happened, logging within the boundaries of the Preserve screeched to a halt. A few corners of the Adirondacks have remained virgin forest as a consequence. Previously logged parts of the Forest Preserve haven't been touched since then, either. That's why there are so many big trees in these woods. They've been allowed to grow old. Eventually, however, the heartwood of an old tree rots to a hollow core and down it comes, blocking the trail.

The Adirondack Mountains aren't the best place for trees to grow old. The topsoil runs shallow in this part of the world. This is largely due to an uplift of rock from deep within the earth and the conspicuous lack of ancient oceanic sediments that cover other places like the Midwest. Thousands of years of freezing and thawing have fractured the Adirondack bedrock into a stony substratum. Trees sink their roots tentatively into this rocky ground. Countless stones, both large and small, weaken the woody grasp of trees, so when a strong wind comes along, even young, healthy ones can topple over without much difficulty.

The DEC, the Adirondack Mountain Club, and a few other hiking organizations do what they can to keep the trails in the Forest Preserve clear, but it's a daunting task, and the trail-clearing crews are pressed to their limits and beyond. Big blowdown will always block the trail. This isn't an altogether bad thing. The way I see it, the bigger the blowdown, the wilder the country. I consider it a privilege to climb over big downed trees or to bushwhack around them. Without such obstacles, my trek would be just another walk through the park.

A PATCH OF RELATIVELY BRIGHT DAYLIGHT filters through the trees. There's some kind of open space ahead. I approach it with just a touch of apprehension. A wetland sprawls north-south across my topographical map, and I expect it to be a somewhat formidable obstacle. All the same, I am not fully prepared for what I encounter a few minutes later. The bog stretches as far as I can see, a quarter mile wide in places. Even its bottleneck, right in front of me, is nearly a hundred yards wide.

The trail across the bog is mostly corduroy—cut logs laid crosswise over wet ground to provide foot support. I step onto the corduroy and am not happy when it gradually sinks beneath dark water. I creep ahead warily, one foot at a time, poking at the submerged boardwalk with my trekking poles to make sure it's still there. On both sides of the unseen boardwalk, patches of sphagnum moss arise from the murky abyss. The prospect of slipping into the drink is very real, so I unbuckle the hip-belt of by pack. I dread crossing the main channel, but the small bridge spanning the deepest part of the wetland rides high above the water's surface. Traversing it is no big deal at all.

In the middle of the wetland, I spot a pair of pitcher plants still in bloom. Their dark red flowers are surprisingly large and healthy-looking for this time of year. I wonder how many unsuspecting insects have fallen into their watery traps, providing these plants with sustenance. A pitcher plant is a bizarre life form. It looks like something that belongs on another planet. It's a sure sign that we live in a curiously diverse world. Life manifests itself in every way imaginable . . . and then some.

When was the last time I saw a pitcher plant? It's been years. They're not uncommon in a place like this, but I don't frequent marshes and bogs the way I used to. Several years ago, after one particularly wet outing, I pulled a bunch of leeches off my legs. That dampened my enthusiasm for wetland exploration. But here I am now so I might as well enjoy it. I stop and take a long second look at the strangely beautiful plants before finishing the crossing. Hard to say when I'll see them again.

By the time I reach the other side of the huge bog, my boots are completely soaked. Not good. My boots are made of hi-tech materials that are both waterproof and breathable, but they aren't designed for wading. So now my feet are wet. That means I'll most likely hobble into camp with blisters tonight. Can't see how that can be avoided.

Shortly after crossing the wetland, I reach Canary Pond. I pass such a sweet-looking campsite nestled beneath conifers that I'm tempted to drop my pack and stay there a while. But no, I have to get as far as the Sacandaga River today if I'm to have any chance of finishing the N-P Trail in the two weeks that I planned to be out here. Ah yes, this is how things always go in deep woods. So many beautiful places, so little time. No matter. I have too much energy to stop moving this early in the day.

I grunt and sweat over a knoll while hiking north. Down the other side, I take a tumble. Even with trekking poles firmly in hand, I lose my footing on a sloped patch of compressed mud and land hard on my side. Rising back to my feet, I scold myself for not being more careful. But being careful only goes so far. This won't be the last time I fall down, I'm sure.

While crossing a small bog a few minutes later, I'm extremely cautious. I move slowly across rotten, moss-covered puncheon. These little wooden bridges laid end-to-end—made up of pairs of flattened, deeply scored logs—effectively keep one's feet out of muck holes and wet places when they're brand new. But they don't age well. Moisture takes its toll on untreated wood, rendering it worse than useless in ten years or so. I hop across the busted middle of one log, leaning hard on my trekking poles in the process. My poles sink deep into the muck on either side of the puncheon. It's a tough crossing, yet I'm grateful for the woodwork all the same. At least I don't have to bushwhack around this bog. That would have been a long detour.

THE NORTHVILLE-PLACID TRAIL is a lowland route. That means it's easy to negotiate for the most part with no big mountains to climb along the way. But thru-hikers shouldn't be fooled by this. As my guidebook points out, the N-P Trail is not for beginners. It's a grand tour of Adirondack wild country. Those who travel it should possess basic first aid, land navigation, and survival skills. Right now, I'm ten miles deep into the Silver Lake Wilderness. If I get lost, injured, or hypothermic out here, I'm in real trouble. And there's no more escape from the elements than the occasional lean-to. In that respect, these woods are more like that wide-open country out west than other wild places here in the Northeast. If I fall down and can't get up on my own, it could be days before anyone comes along to help me. Big woods. I ponder this while stepping gingerly around muck holes that I would usually ignore.

Big woods or no, the surrounding landscape looks quite familiar to me. It's much like the wilder parts of the Green Mountains in my native Vermont. While skirting the half-drained remnant of a large beaver pond, I spot a patch of black raspberries just like those back home. I stop to eat a few before going any farther. Another patch appears a short while later so I eat a few more. They are well past their prime. I don't care. I consume a handful of them before crossing the pond's outlet stream and slipping back into the shady forest. Most thru-hikers wouldn't waste their time collecting and eating wild berries, I suppose. After all, a bag of trail mix provides many times more energy than any mere handful of berries. But I can't pass up berries ripe for the picking.

So precious and ephemeral, wild berries are gifts from the gods to be sure. In a way they represent all that's right with the world. They help keep the cycle of life in motion. Although their sudden appearance always seems like a windfall, they exist because of creatures like me. Their seeds quickly pass through a bird or animal's body and are deposited on the ground with ample fertilizer, just as intended. Picking and eating them reminds me that I can play a small role in wild nature as well as any other creature. My stomach has no trouble processing this uncultivated food. In fact, I could live out here indefinitely if I had to, eating berries, roots, fish, grubs, and small animals just as my distant ancestors did. That's a pleasant thought. So I wear the purplish stains proudly while I hike.

Chapter 3

THE SUN BREAKS THROUGH the drab overcast sky, illuminating the forest floor, brightening the green, yellow, and orange leaves in the canopy overhead. The mere sight of so much brilliant color lifts my spirits, justifying all the effort it has taken to get this deep into the woods. But my elation doesn't last. In the next moment, a dark cloud rolls overhead, dropping its load. The shower ends just as quickly as it started, but the forest remains dripping wet and misty in subdued light. Oh well. Over the years, I've learned to take such things in stride. Rain comes and goes. Both sky and moods change.

The amphibious creatures beneath my feet see things differently. Frogs, toads, and red efts revel in the sudden dampness. This is their idea of a good day, and they come out by the thousands to celebrate. They're all over these woods. They're scattered all over the muddy trail. To keep from crushing them, I have to be careful about where I step.

Several white, phallic-looking mushrooms catch my eye as I amble down the trail. I spot a large patch of bright orange fungus, then a few small toadstools, then a greasy brown patch of I-don't-know-what. I see puffballs thriving in the rotting corpse of a tree; nod to the woody shelf mushrooms clinging to beech tree trunks like so many cancerous growths; wince at the rather alien-looking, bright yellow fingers protruding from forest debris. How strange can nature get? Very strange, it seems, when it comes to fungus.

Mushrooms pop up all over the place this time of year. They assume every shape, texture, and size. I've seen "elephant ears" bigger than a bucket and other mushrooms smaller than a thumbnail. Yellow, tan, cream, red, orange, even purple—they come in every color of the rainbow. Every color, that is, but green. No, not green. Green, after all, is the color of chlorophyll, which mushrooms do not produce. They get what they need of that vital substance from other plants. And there is no shortage of donors.

To be sure, mushrooms are an essential part of nature's demolition crew. Looking around me, I am amazed by the profusion of dead and dying trees slowly being dismantled by them. With considerable help from bugs and bacteria, they break down everything that touches the ground, as well as the few trunks of dead trees still standing upright. The forest is full of fungi, especially in a wet year like this one, especially on a wet day like today. If you don't like the look of mushrooms, then you shouldn't be in the woods at summer's end. They are as much a part of this damp, shady world as ferns and mosses are. It's hard to imagine how this woody world could regenerate without their help.

Which ones are edible? Which ones are poisonous? I don't know. That's why I've never picked and eaten a wild mushroom in all my years of backcountry travel. I spot what I believe to be a member of the dreadful *amanita* family—those relatively normal-looking mushrooms that will make you suffer terribly before killing you. I think that's what I'm looking at, anyhow. Can't say for sure. Some mushrooms belong in the pantry, others in the pharmacy. Still others should be left alone. I marvel at those who can harvest wild mushrooms with supreme confidence. How do they do it? Years of careful study with someone who knows, I suppose. Trial and error is certainly the wrong way to go.

JUST BEFORE REACHING MUD LAKE, I stop by a brook to refill my two liter-sized bottles. The water filter that I'm using has a brand new cartridge in it so the task goes quickly. As I work, a sunbeam catches me in the act. Light glances off the shallow stream, blinding me with its shimmering brilliance. I look away but the sun's heat still caresses my face. A few moments later, I bask in the sunlight while slaking my thirst. The beautiful, unfamiliar melody of an unseen songbird fills the forest. I hear the delicate tinkle of a brook that has been flowing longer than human beings have been civilized. I listen to it while water drips from my beard. Then I stuff both water bottles into my pack and go.

Midday, a mile farther down the trail, I drop my pack on the planked floor of the Mud Lake lean-to. I'm glad to have it off my back for a while. Time for lunch. I pull out maps, a food bag, and my journal. A monarch butterfly flutters through the tall grass nearby. Goldenrod blooms in all its late-summer glory, accompanied by blue and white asters. I see a few bright orange touch-me-nots also flowering in the mix. What other wildflowers have I seen so far? Half a mile back, I noticed a white, translucent protrusion called Indian pipe growing on the forest floor. I recall a solitary turtlehead flower bowing to me from a low wet spot earlier in the day. Not much else. The procession of wildflowers that began so dramatically with trilliums and trout lilies last spring is now coming to a quiet end. Compared to that riotous outburst of color earlier in the year, the autumn bloom is rather subtle and unassuming.

Beyond Mud Lake, the trail ascends to a notch in a low ridge. The landscape changes significantly on the other side of it. This part of the forest, thinned by logging, is bright and airy. The ground slopes gently towards the Sacandaga River. While meandering through this broadleaf forest in the long afternoon, I ponder something Ralph Waldo Emerson wrote in his journal over a hundred and fifty years ago: "A walk in the woods is only an exalted dream." Like so much of what that old Yankee philosopher said about our interaction with wild nature, it has the ring of truth to it. There is something about a daylong hike through this green infinity that's mesmerizing. There's something romantic about it, as well—romantic in the truest sense of the word. Romantic with a capital "R."

THE DESERT WILDERNESS WAS a desolate, unwelcome place in biblical times. Prophets entered it only to test their spiritual mettle. It wasn't good for much else. Before he started his ministry, Jesus of Nazareth ventured into the desert to fast and pray. The gospel report about how the Devil tempted Jesus during his wilderness wandering made perfect sense to those living two thousand years ago. The wilderness was, after all, the Devil's playground.

During the seventeenth century, zealous Christian missionaries ventured deep into the dark, unbroken forests of North America. French priests like Isaac Jogues carried the word of God to the native people there. They took great risks by doing so. The natives did not always welcome them with open arms. Besides, the wilderness itself had a corrosive effect upon one's moral character, or so many of the priests believed. As Father Jogues concluded, this wild country was as hostile to Christian virtues as the Iroquois "demons" who had captured and tortured him. Seen through his eyes, the Adirondack Mountains were bastions of godlessness. Surely no good could ever come from them.

The Puritans, settling in the country just east of the Adirondacks, had no illusions about what lurked beyond their wooden forts. They were quick to cut down trees and harness the land. The Puritans pushed back the wilderness, along with all the terrible beasts and wild people in it, until it no longer posed a threat to them. In due time, they tamed this country. They called it New England and put most of its tillable soil to good use.

Then and only then did attitudes towards wilderness change.

Early in the nineteenth century, a tightly knit group of freethinking Yankees in the Boston area cultivated a fresh, new worldview. Heavily influenced by English Romantic poets like Wordsworth and German Idealist thinkers like Goethe and Kant, they redefined humankind's relationship to nature. They called themselves Transcendentalists and preached a "higher law"—rooted in the natural world—that went beyond all societal mores. Ralph Waldo Emerson placed himself at the forefront of this movement when he published a slender volume called *Nature*. His protégé, Henry David Thoreau, emerged as one of the movement's most eloquent spokesmen. As Roderick Nash points out in his book, *Wilderness and the American Mind*, the Transcendentalists completely reversed Puritan notions about the wild, arguing "that one's chances of attaining moral perfection and knowing God were *maximized* by entering wilderness."

In 1836, the same year that Emerson's *Nature* was published, a professor of Geology named Ebenezer Emmons climbed Mount Marcy—the highest peak in the Adirondacks. He did this with the help of a backcountry guide, John Cheney. A bit later, Cheney led the newspaperman Charles Fenno Hoffman into the Adirondacks, as well. Thanks to Emmons, Hoffman and people like them, word soon got out that these wild and beautiful mountains were only a few days north of the nation's large, bustling, east coast cities. And while land-hungry Americans remained focused upon that wide-open country out west, Thomas Cole and a few other artists painted their way up the Hudson River, drawing considerable attention to the Adirondacks. As a consequence, these mountains came to represent wild nature at its most glorious and sublime.

The die had been cast by the time Emerson and nine other notable thinkers sojourned briefly at the "Philosopher's Camp" on Follensbee Pond, in the heart of the Adirondacks. That gathering took place in 1858.

Shortly thereafter, hordes of nature-lovers flocked to the mountains in search of the "exalted dream" about which Emerson, Cole, and those like them were writing and painting. And the word "wilderness," once associated with dark, sinister forces, took on a brand new meaning.

LATE AFTERNOON. The West Branch of the Sacandaga River pops into view soon after my ears catch the first sound of rushing water. I cross the long suspension footbridge, imagining someone on the other side greeting me the way that supporters greet marathon runners at a finish line. It's been a long, nine-mile hike to this point, and my body is feeling it. I drop my pack in a grassy clearing at the northern end of the footbridge. An old stone chimney still stands in the clearing—the remnant of some old hunting camp. It's time for an energy bar and a little water.

I hobble down to the stream's edge to take a picture of both the bridge and the river, somewhat surprised that they won't fit in the camera's viewfinder. It's hard to believe that a stream this big flows through the middle of nowhere. Where is the river coming from? Where is it going? Both ends of it run off my map. In that regard, a big patch of open country like Silver Lake Wilderness can be somewhat unsettling. There seems to be no connection between where I am right now and the rest of the world. It's a very strange feeling.

The "No Camping" sign tacked to a nearby tree reminds me that I've got to start thinking about where I'm going to sleep tonight. So far I've been hiking smart, not setting any goals for the day, allowing my body to tell me how far it wants to go. Right now my body is telling me that it's time to call it quits. The Hamilton Lake Stream lean-to, recommended by my guidebook, is still two miles away. Two miles can feel like a great distance—much more than I care to undertake at this point, anyhow. So I hoist the heavy pack to my sore shoulders and resume my march, looking for a place nearby to make camp.

Shortly after the river disappears behind me, I reach a "T" trail junction. I turn left, following blue NPT markers pointing northwest. The trail runs parallel to the river for a while. I glance through the trees on my left, looking for a flat, relatively clear spot next to the river. But this is a flood plain, so I'm hesitant to camp here. By the time I've reached higher ground, the trail has veered far away from the river. Oh well. I'll just have to make camp next to the first feeder stream that comes along. The contours on my map assure me that there must be one not too far ahead. Sure enough, I find a tiny rivulet a few minutes later, but the ground around it is uneven and boggy. Now what?

I drop my pack and study my map, reassessing the situation. It's late in the afternoon. There's about an hour and a half of daylight left. I've come ten miles today, and the sore spots on my feet tell me that I'm dangerously close to getting blisters. I should stop and patch my feet, but that would take time. I'm tired. A few minutes ago, I fell down again. Should make camp here even though this isn't the best place to do so. On the other hand, that lean-to is only a mile away . . .

I reach the Hamilton Lake Stream lean-to just before the sunset. Way too tired to collect wood or build a fire, I draw just enough water to get me through the night. Then I fire up my camp stove. Dinner is a hurried affair. I sling my food bags in the trees right before the last twilight fades. Once that's done, I strip off my clothes and check my legs as well as my feet. Not good. I have a thumb-sized blister on the ball of my right foot and a few toes have been rubbed raw. I also have some serious chafing on my inner thighs, where wet clothes have been irritating my skin for the past two days. Two spots are bleeding. Hmm. Not good at all. Today's eleven-mile trek has exacted a heavy toll. So much for hiking smart.

Chapter 4

TUESDAY, SEPTEMBER 5TH. Third day in the woods. I awaken to the constant *meep-meep* of a nuthatch. I look at my watch and am shocked to find that it's past seven already. I've slept over ten hours. Must have needed it. The aches, pains, and stiffness throughout my body confirm this as I crawl from my sleeping bag. Definitely feeling fifty years old this morning—fifty going on sixty. I hiked way too far yesterday.

First things first: patch feet, toes, and inner thighs before getting dressed. Mosquitoes buzz around my head while I'm doing this, as if to remind me that it's still summer. I wave them away while focusing on the particularly nasty-looking blister on the bottom of my right foot. Hmm. Could force me off the trail. All depends upon how bad it gets. I pull out moleskin, band-aids, and triple antibiotic ointment, then set to work. Walking around in my boots afterward, I can hardly feel the blister. Good. With any luck, the patch will keep it from getting worse.

While drawing water for breakfast, I hear a loud crash in the woods across the stream. Moments later, I hear the distinct sound of something big pushing through the undergrowth. Twigs snap and leaves rustle. I peer deep into the misty forest, looking for a flash of grey, brown, or black fur. Nothing. A limb cracks loudly, ruling out grey. Too big to be a deer. So what is it then, a bear or a moose? I retreat to the shelter and boil up water on my camp stove while pondering the matter, still searching the forest edge along the stream for a glimpse of fur. Still nothing. When finally the sound fades into the distance, I'm just a tad disappointed. Half expected a moose to pop into view. While bears are more common than moose in the Adirondacks, that familiar crashing sound has been a prelude to seeing moose on other occasions. Why not this time?

Rumor has it that moose have returned in force to the Adirondacks during the past couple decades. Not just the occasional animal wandering in from New England where they thrive, but permanent residents. This makes sense. The moose population has been exploding in Vermont since the early eighties. One doesn't need a degree in wildlife biology to imagine a few dozen of them to migrating around the lower end of Lake Champlain. That would put them right here, in the "Great South Woods" of the Adirondacks, where a large number of deer already live. Moose have been seen regularly around Indian Lake, not twenty miles north of here as the bird flies. But some wildlife biologists maintain that the last moose was hunted out of the Adirondacks well over a hundred years ago and attempts to reintroduce them since then have failed. The return of the moose is only wishful thinking, they'll tell you, based on the rare sightings of strays. But ask anyone living in the southern Adirondacks and they'll tell you that moose are here to stay.

Back on the trail, I search the mud holes for large, hoofed tracks but find nothing. No bear or deer tracks either. Just the prints of The Trekker and Pip deeply embedded in mud, relentlessly pressing northward. I follow them through the woods, across a stream, and past a rather large wetland called Priests Vly. The cool morning air makes hiking easy. I maintain a good clip—two miles an hour, at least—excited by the prospect of reaching Piseco before noon. It's only a few miles away. I look forward to resupplying in Piseco. And it'll be nice to talk with someone again, however briefly. In the meantime, I ponder the subtle beauty of the forest around me, wondering if anyone in that first great wave of visitors coming here over a hundred years ago saw this country the way I do now.

A FEW ADVENTUROUS SOULS traveled to the Adirondacks during the middle of the nineteenth century, but tourists didn't really start flocking here in great numbers until after the Civil War. In 1869, Reverend William H.H. Murray published a book called *Adventures in the Wilderness*, creating a flurry of interest in the region. His book was an overnight bestseller. Coming as it did on the heels of the Industrial Revolution, it was the right book at the right time. Urbanites weary from the endless clang of industry were hungry for some kind of release. And that's exactly what Murray's North Woods promised.

Not only did Adirondack scenery rival the Swiss Alps, a trip into the mountains could "restore impaired health." That's what Murray claimed, anyhow. More importantly, a trip into the wilderness could rejuvenate the spirit. He called on ministers everywhere to follow his example and retreat to the woods. "In the wilderness they would find that perfect relaxation which all jaded minds require," he wrote. Thanks to Murray, people were soon heading to the Adirondacks by the trainload.

Newspaper writers called them "Murray's Fools" because the vast majority of those arriving in the Adirondack hotels at this time had absolutely no idea what they were getting themselves into. Most assumed that all they needed to do was hire a guide for a few days and all the benefits of wild nature would magically land in their laps. In his book Murray had played down the hardships of backcountry travel, so many pilgrims quickly became disenchanted by the harsh realities of the wild. Few of them anticipated the utter lack of amenities, the physical exertion, the dirt, rain, and bloodthirsty insects. The summer of 1869 was especially wet and buggy. That didn't help matters.

Disgruntled pilgrims called Murray a liar. During the 1870s, he rose to his own defense. He worked the lecture circuit, tirelessly promoting the benefits of wilderness travel. And with a little help from the writings of Henry David Thoreau, George Perkins Marsh, and other nature enthusiasts, Murray managed to squelch the criticism somewhat—among those who attended his lectures, anyhow. But his credibility as a writer was blown.

Despite bad press early on, the Adirondacks remained a popular travel destination in the decades that followed. Improved rail access to the region helped, as did the sudden appearance of sanitariums, where ailing city-dwellers could go to breathe the pure mountain air. The rising tide of romantically inclined tourists couldn't be stopped by the omissions and exaggerations of one rather sentimental minister. Times and attitudes had changed. As Paul Schneider put it so well in his book, *The Adirondacks*: "Two centuries after Isaac Jogues encountered his Iroquois 'demons,' the park had become one of the residences of God." Yesterday's forbidding wilderness was today's sanctuary. The wasteland was now paradise.

CLOSED GENTIAN, MEADOWSWEET AND GOLDENROD bloom in the overgrown field through which I pass after exiting the shadowy forest. The sky overhead seems exceptionally bright despite a seamless, grey canopy of clouds. The light from it makes me squint. A few minutes later, I am standing on the edge of a paved road—Route 8—looking for a gas station or general store. I spot one a hundred yards up the road and immediately head in that direction. My trekking poles make a loud clicking sound as they knock against the asphalt. A truck roars past and it's all I can do to keep from flinching. I feel exposed in this treeless expanse.

"Need a ride?" someone asks me right before I reach the store. I turn around to see the big smile of a young, pretty woman in a little blue car. No, I don't need a ride, but I'm ready to strike up a conversation with her, anyway. There's another young woman in the passenger's seat, so I squat down next to the car to make eye contact with her, as well. Once I tell them that I'm a thru-hiker—which is what they suspected when they saw me crossing the road—they inquire about trail conditions in the Silver Lake Wilderness. They intend to hike the NPT as soon as they link up with another friend of theirs. The three of them will set forth from the Benson trailhead, following my footsteps this far, at least. The two bulging backpacks on the back seat of their car attest to their earnestness, so I tell them everything I know.

I pull out my map, occasionally pointing to it while I talk. I tell them all about the mud holes, downed trees, submerged sections of trail, rotten puncheon and bogs. "Sounds worse than it is," I add as an afterthought. Then I tout the wild beauty of it all, recommending that they camp at Canary Pond if they can. The Silver Lake Wilderness is well worth the effort necessary to traverse it, I assure them. To drive this point home, I tell the bright-eyed young women that the only real hardship I've suffered has been hobo coffee. "Forgot to pack coffee filters," I say rather sheepishly while nodding towards the store, "but I intend to pick up some in there in a few minutes."

"Whenever I go into the woods," the driver says, "I carry a French press." A good cup off coffee isn't something she's willing to do without. The press is a little bulky, she admits, but well worth the extra weight. And with that tidbit of information, I scratch off the possibility of them catching up to me at West Canada Lake. They don't seem like the kind of people who can shrug off the countless small hardships of backcountry travel for more than a couple days at a time. Then again, they could be real hiking machines—who knows? I wish them good luck as we part ways.

Inside the store, a short, squat fellow informs me that they're out of coffee filters. Then, in the next breath, he asks how many I need. A half dozen or so will get me to Long Lake, I tell him. He goes over to the coffee counter near the window and counts out eight filters. Then he hands them to me. I offer to pay for the filters but he refuses my money. I thank him twice over, grabbing a bag of tortilla chips and a soda from the shelves to pay for instead.

A second, much larger man enters the store just as I'm cashing out. He wheels around the counter and barks: "Is that your backpack out there on the bench?" When I respond that it is, he tells me not to sit in the cushioned chairs next to the bench. He doesn't want my dirt and sweat all over his nice, clean chairs. I laugh nervously at this, somewhat surprised by his gruff manner. But the big, burly fellow doesn't think it's funny, so I muster as much seriousness as I can while assuring him that I intend to keep moving. Then I wish both men a good day. Outside, while walking away from the store, I'm just a tad distressed by his insinuation. I'm not *that* dirty, am I? I put on a clean t-shirt this morning before coming to town. I'll bet he didn't even notice.

IT'S A TWO-MILE ROAD WALK from Route 8 to the Piseco Post Office, which is the closest thing to a town center that this community has. I keep to the sandy shoulder of the road to lessen the wear and tear on my feet. A few locals zoom past in pickups and SUVs. I stop by a stream flowing into Piseco Lake to chow down some of the chips and soda that I just bought. After that I resume my walk. It takes the better part of an hour to reach the post office. No matter. I've got all day.

The post office is closed for lunch by the time I'm standing in front of it. I have a box of supplies inside so I'll just have to wait for it to reopen. Time to break for lunch, anyway. I drop my pack in the grass next to the post office and open it. Out comes what's left of the chips and soda, along with my food bag and water bottle. Out comes the card I'll mail to Judy this afternoon. I pen a few lines in it. Crickets serenade me while I eat and write.

When the post office reopens, I retrieve one of the two boxes of food that I popped in the mail a week and a half ago. Another one is waiting for me at the Long Lake post office about sixty miles north. In this box, there's only a two-day supply of food. Happy to have the extra provisions for the big wilderness crossing directly ahead, I load it all into my pack. Then I ask the clerk behind the counter if she could take the empty box off my hands. No problem, she tells me. She snaps up the box with a great big smile. I just love small town post offices. The smaller they are, the nicer the people running them.

I FOLLOW A SET OF DEER TRACKS pressed deep into the soft shoulder of the dead-end road while making my way back to the woods. One last mile of open ground between the post office and the trailhead and then I'm home free. The road narrows as it changes from asphalt to dirt. The limited contact that I've just had with "civilization" will have to sustain me during the next few days. I'm sure it will. As I've learned on previous excursions, a little contact goes a long way.

I feel like a walking supermarket. I've added four more pounds of food to the sixteen pounds I had in my pack at the Benson trailhead. How much have I consumed during the past two and a half days? About three or four pounds, so it's a wash, really. All the same, I feel loaded. That's a good thing, I suppose. I'm just about to enter one of the largest patches of wild country east of the Mississippi. It'll be four or five days before I pop out the other side, then another three days before I pick up the next parcel. An eight-day supply of food isn't too much to be carrying.

According to the trailhead register, The Trekker and his dog are three days ahead of me now. They're moving fast. No doubt he'll hike the entire

NPT in his allotted nine days. As for me, well, I intend to cut my pace, hike even more slowly. I intend to savor the West Canada Lakes Wilderness and the corner of Jessup River Wild Forest I'll pass through before reaching it. The big roadless area directly ahead is the main event of this trek. I enter it with a great big smile. Yessir, Adirondack wildness at its finest.

A ruffed grouse meanders slowly across the trail, seemingly indifferent to my presence. How odd. Once I catch up to her, she stops in the brush and turns sideways to check me out. We stare at each other for several minutes, with no more than five yards of broken ground between us. This is one grouse that won't live long, I keep thinking. It's not afraid of humans. Then again, I don't know the whole story. Maybe there aren't any bird hunters around here to take advantage of her unwariness. I nod towards the old bird, wishing her the best, then resume my hike.

A mile down the trail, I step across a pretty little feeder stream. It's even nicer than I thought it would be when I first located it on my map. Yes, this will do quite nicely. I bushwhack fifty yards upstream, getting just far enough away from the trail to disappear from view. Then I drop my pack. This'll be my home for the night. It's three o'clock in the afternoon. I could hike for another hour or two but I see no point in it. Still sore from yesterday's eleven mile slog, I figure that eight miles is enough today. Besides, I've got that blister on my foot to consider. Don't want it getting any worse.

It takes about an hour to set up my tarp, sling food in the trees, create a small campfire circle with fist-sized stones, and gather wood. That's all I ever need to do in order to turn an unremarkable patch of forest floor into a sweet little camp. After I clean up, I make a journal entry. Harassing mosquitoes convince me to start a fire long before it's time to cook dinner. The smoke keeps them at bay. I squirrel away just enough wood to boil up water for coffee tomorrow morning, then gather a little more for a campfire reverie later on this evening. After that, I lean back against a birch tree and enjoy the surrounding forest. For the first time in three days, I sit tight for hours on end—looking around, listening, quite comfortable just being here. It's a welcome break from continuous movement.

Chapter 5

THE HIGH-PITCHED CACKLE of a pileated woodpecker jars me awake. I open my eyes to a golden dawn filtering through the trees—the promise of a beautiful day. Mosquitoes whine a few inches above my face, frustrated by netting that hangs down from the tarp. Good thing I fixed that netting into place before settling into bed last night. I slept well because of it, despite the constant buzzing of mosquitoes and an unseen rodent rummaging around camp. My flashlight attempts to scare away that fleet-footed little creature didn't really work. At one point it ran across the tarp, directly over my head. Where's an owl when you need one?

Crawling out of bed and getting dressed takes considerable effort. Down by the stream, I splash cold water on my face to wake up. A half hour slips away before I'm alert enough to retrieve food bags from the trees and get breakfast started. I build a fire about the size of a pie pan. It's only a flash of heat—all that's necessary to boil a small pot of water. No fanfare. Just a cooking fire. I let it burn down to a handful of embers while sipping coffee and making plans. Today I'm going all the way to Spruce Lake. Not a great distance—only nine miles—but far enough.

I check the clothes hanging from parachute cord strung between two trees. The underwear and socks that I held over the campfire last night are completely dry now, but everything else is still a little damp. Yeah, the underwear and socks are dry, all right—toasted to a light brown. Daylight reveals what campfire light could not. Held them just a bit too close to the flame. Oh well. I'll wear them anyway.

I douse the embers before finishing my coffee, then take my time breaking camp. I scatter unused firewood across the forest floor, drop the tarp and slowly pack up. I patch my feet before ripping off the oversized bandages covering the raw spots on my inner thighs. Good news: the big blister on the bottom of my right foot hasn't gotten any worse. More good news: the raw spot on my right thigh has completely healed. But when I tear off the bandage covering the raw spot on my left thigh, a quarter-inch piece of skin comes away with it. Ouch! Now I have an even worse spot to contend with. It'll be a job keeping it from getting infected.

After rolling a mat of forest duff over the black scar where the campfire was, I brush the ground with a spruce bough to hide my footprints. Then I'm ready to go. Pack to shoulders, hip belt snapped, trekking poles in hand. One last look at Piseco camp before I tramp back to the trail. It's slow going at first, but after a quick leg stretch I'm soon making tracks. Today I'm hiking deeper into the forest. There's nothing else on my itinerary. Today I'm a woodswalker, pure and simple.

The trail turns sharply to the west as it begins to climb. I stop in a small notch just long enough to down half a liter of water and a couple handfuls of trail mix. Then I'm on the move again. I catch a glimpse of light through the trees to the north. The large wetland over there never really comes into full view, but I see enough light to know it exists. A few large, muddy spots crop up, but the trail is high and dry for the most part. In a forest like this, the word "muddy" is relative, of course. If my boots don't sink at least an inch into muck, I consider the ground dry.

After a quick descent, I reach Fall Stream. It looks like a good place to take a long break so I drop my pack. It's a good place to listen to chickadees, watch the occasional mayfly rise from rushing water, and get in tune with the wild, anyhow. Hmm…the wild. Like so many nature lovers, I put "the" in front of "wild" to give it more weight, to draw attention to something important. But what am I talking about? What is *the wild*, really?

The wild is that intangible, unnamable Otherness that's so pervasive out here. I see it in the green infinity all around me. I hear it in the deep forest silence. It smells like ozone, wet moss, wildflowers, and something decaying. It excites all my senses yet remains imperceptible, ever elusive, mystical. It's something raw and unfettered. It's what motivates people like me to come out here time and again, despite the mud, bugs, rain, and countless other hardships. For lack of better words, I call it *the wild*, as many woodswalkers have before me. I could give a dozen good reasons for coming out here, but none of them would hold up to careful scrutiny. Not really. It's the wild and the wild only that keeps me coming back. She's my mistress, my goddess, my very reason for being. Without her, I would slowly suffocate in my own miserable abstractions. Without her, I would cease being fully human.

A CLEAR PLASTIC COMPASS dangles from a lanyard slung around my neck whenever I'm in the woods. When someone asks me what it is, I say, "hiker's jewelry." When accompanied by a hearty laugh, this answer usually keeps me from ranting and raving at some poor, unsuspecting stranger about the importance of knowing where you are. The blatant disregard that most people have for land navigation irks me to no end. Whenever I read in the newspaper about a hiker getting lost, I go crazy. Nine times out of ten, there's no good reason for it.

Some hikers rely solely upon trail markers to get around. Others use maps, which work well as long as they're detailed, up-to-date, and properly oriented. Still others employ "a sense of direction," whatever that's supposed to be. Nowadays, high-tech hikers carry Global Positioning

Systems, which are electronic devices that use satellites orbiting high above the earth to pinpoint locations on the ground. An ex-military friend of mine pulls out his GPS whenever we hike together and it seems to work quite well. But whenever I'm alone, I prefer something that doesn't require batteries. I'd rather use a simple, old-fashioned, low-tech compass.

A compass hanging from my neck is a constant reminder that wilderness travel is serious business, and I check it on a regular basis, despite the fact that I've been tramping around the woods since I was ten years old. In this regard, *the wild* is very tangible, indeed. North, south, east, west—if you don't know what direction you're going, you're either lost or on the verge of becoming so. With that in mind, I carry the tools necessary to get around in the woods, both map and compass. And I know how to use them.

I love wild nature and am strongly attracted to it, but I keep my romantic notions in their proper place. I know how to negotiate the forest without the benefit of a trail. I also know how to take care of myself in most situations. In my pack at all times there's a first aid kit, plenty of matches, water purification tablets, and dry clothes. And it's all wrapped in plastic. I might daydream while hiking through the woods, but I'm ready for any challenge that comes my way. It's a strange mindset, this unlikely mix of romanticism and practicality, but it works out here in the woods. To be sure, it separates this forest life from that rather mundane existence back in the developed lowlands.

EARLY AFTERNOON. While approaching a small pond that's unnamed on my map, I spot a golden toad hopping away from the trail. I saw a tan frog a couple hours ago that wasn't more than an inch long. Near the marshy pond, a bright orange frog glows beneath the conifers. What's with all these strange-looking amphibians? Soon I find some typically green frogs, along with a few brownish toads. All the same, it feels like I'm traveling through some forgotten world where bizarre creatures abound. Or is the persistent dampness only making common animals more visible? Either way, I am humbled by my own ignorance. Just when I think I've got the forest all figured out, some small plant or animal takes me by surprise. It happens almost every time I come out here. Fact is, I'm not half the naturalist I think I am.

The trail gradually descends to the Jessup River, and I'm a little concerned about what I'll find when I reach it. There's no bridge across the Jessup and, according to my guidebook, the ford can be dicey when the water's running high. When finally I see the broad, shallow stream crossing, I shake my head and laugh. It's no big deal at all. Someone has strategically placed rocks across the stream, making it a cinch to traverse. My boots barely get wet as I skip across. I've encountered mud holes that were more daunting.

On the other side of the river, I refill my water bottles. Then I take on a rather steep stretch of trail. I spot more toads and frogs during the climb—a clear case of seeing what one expects to see. There are lots of blue asters, as well. They bloom along the edges of what was once a logging trail. The big grey square on my map tells the story. Some logging outfit owns this part of the forest, or must have owned it not long ago. But when the trail veers to the west, narrowing considerably, there's no doubt in my mind that I've ventured beyond the reach of skidders and chainsaws. I'm entering the West Canada Lakes Wilderness. I somehow missed the sign announcing it, but the land around me is indisputably wild now, and the trail twisting through it is no logger's highway.

Immediately after crossing Bloodgood Brook, I notice claw marks on the trunks of beech trees. Lots and lots of claw marks. This is the first hard evidence of bear activity I've seen so far. It's late afternoon now, getting towards evening. Keep my eyes open and I just might catch one coming out to play. Although bears are nocturnal for the most part, they're usually up and moving around by dusk.

I've gained six hundred feet in elevation since leaving my camp north of Piseco this morning, and the trail is still climbing. When it levels out, I stop to catch my breath. I flush a large deer out of the brush shortly thereafter. Only then do I notice the many deer tracks pressed into the mud underfoot. They point every which way. There must be a dozen deer on this knoll. Maybe more. I wonder who else lives here. I pull out my watch. Five o'clock. There are only a couple hours of daylight left. Good thing Spruce Lake is less than a mile away.

The trail drops down into a dark, dense stand of conifers covering a large, wet, somewhat flat stretch of ground. Rough going. At the end of the day, with my pack feeling twice as heavy as it did this morning, it's hard staying on my feet. I roll my ankle once. I laugh while shaking it out. I roll it again. Whenever people ask me what Vermont's Long Trail is like, I say it's the trail of a hundred summits. Conversely, I'd call the NPT the trail of a hundred ponds and wetlands. But it feels more like the trail of a thousand mud holes right now. Good thing the NPT isn't all like this. Dodging mud holes, constantly hopping back and forth between roots and rocks, is not my idea of a good time.

As a direct result of the Industrial Revolution, which kicked into high gear during the mid-1800s, attitudes towards nature changed. As attitudes changed, so did values. All of a sudden people started thinking about protecting America's wild places. In 1872, Yellowstone Park was created. About the same time, there was talk of establishing a similar preserve in northern New York. In anticipation, the New York State Legislature commissioned Verplanck Colvin to survey the Adirondack Mountains. That survey proved to be just the thing needed to get the preservation movement going in the East.

Verplanck Colvin was the right man at the right time. He was one of the most outspoken advocates for forest preservation, and his surveying adventures drew considerable attention to the Adirondacks. The same year he was made chief surveyor, he traced the source of the Hudson River to a small alpine lake nestled in the lap of Mount Marcy. He called it Lake Tear-of-the-Clouds. The name stuck, Colvin's voice grew louder, and soon New Yorkers were taking very seriously his call for a forest preserve in the Adirondacks.

Colvin's argument for forest preservation came straight from the writings of George Perkins Marsh. In 1864, Marsh published the conservation classic, *Man and Nature*. In that book he established a link between human activity and water—the most valuable of all natural resources. Marsh reasoned that wild forests are the wellsprings of river systems. Unrestricted logging turns these wild forests into virtual deserts, thereby threatening the availability and flow of water. In a time when most shipping was done by waterways, a threat of this sort cut right to the heart of what mattered most, namely commerce. "With the disappearance of the forest," Marsh wrote, "all is changed." And nearly everyone agreed that a change of this sort wouldn't be for the best.

Thanks to the visionary work of Marsh, Colvin, and others like them, the New York State Legislature passed a law in 1885 creating Forest Preserves in both the Catskills and the Adirondacks. By then the State of New York had been quietly acquiring land for over a decade. In the nineteenth century, it was a common practice for logging companies to default on the property taxes due for a parcel of land once they had harvested the best trees from it. When they defaulted, the State seized the land. Later on the State would sell it back to the lumber companies at a fraction of its value. Things went on like this for a long time. As a consequence of this dubious arrangement, the State was holding almost 700,000 acres of timberland when the Forest Preserves were created. And that was the first land to become "forever wild."

THE LEAN-TO LOCATED AT the southernmost end of Spruce Lake pops into view the moment I climb out of the mud bogs. It's a dark, rather dismal-looking place beneath a stand of old spruces. It's also littered with trash. There's no view of the lake, either. I'm not keen about staying here tonight, but it's getting late and the clouds overhead are thickening. Besides, I'm tired. I drop my pack inside the lean-to while pondering the matter. A thin drizzle commences a moment later and that settles it. I declare the lean-to my home for the night and immediately set to work picking up the trash. After that, I go looking for the lake.

Spruce Lake is a wild, beautiful place. Too bad the lean-to is a hundred yards away. I snap a photo of the lake from a small clearing on its shoreline, wondering how the two boats got here. The rowboat has a patch in it; the canoe is well worn. They've both been here a while. Many years, I'd say. Probably brought here by amphibious plane before this part of the forest was designated a wilderness area. That's my guess, anyhow. Can't imagine anyone hauling these boats over the rough trail that I just hiked, but you never know.

Back in camp, I eat a quick dinner, then sling my food bags high in the trees. I'm thinking ahead. West Lake, located right in the middle of this huge wilderness, is only a day's hike away. Even more than hiking the Northville-Placid Trail end-to-end, I want to reach that lake. It's something I wanted to do four years ago, when a particularly nasty blister on my foot cut short a hike from the north. If the bears get my food tonight, I'll be foiled again. Haven't lost food to bears in all my years of backpacking, but it happens to other hikers often enough. I hoist my food bags farther off the ground than I usually would. If the gods are willing, I'll be camped at West Lake tomorrow night. No big deal, really, but I'd like to see that lake. It's something to think about while settling in for the night, anyhow.

Chapter 6

THE LOONS THAT CALLED all night long are silent at daybreak. In their place I hear the staccato chatter of squirrels and the steady *thump!* of red spruce cones hitting the forest floor. I also hear a light rain falling. Listening more intently, I notice something peculiar about those dripping sounds. Occasionally, a much fainter *plunk!* is audible among the raindrops. I think those are beechnuts coming down.

I had a strange dream last night—one that's out of context, anyway. While nestled in a warm sleeping bag with my eyes still closed, I sort through what I can recall, trying to reconstruct the storyline. I was in a bistro or café, in the company of several beautiful women, somewhere in a big, foreign city. Paris maybe. The waiter spoke French. The bistro was dark and the rhythmic music playing in the background was vaguely erotic. That's all I remember. But it's enough underscore the dramatic difference between where I was last night and where I am now.

Thump! There goes another spruce cone.

"Life in the woods is a fiction," Alain once said. "The man of the woods is a fugitive." In my mind's eye, I can see that French philosopher sitting in a Parisian café, surveying the urban landscape around him, casually turning to an attentive companion to make that assertion. He is scoffing at me, scoffing at my romantic idea of forest redemption. To him the "Green Man," the woods wanderer perfectly tuned to the wild, is no more real than Santa Claus or the Easter Bunny. And all those mystical notions about "the wild" don't hold up in the cold, hard light of reason. In short, they are myths conjured up by outsiders like me to make us feel better, perhaps even self-righteous, about being alienated from society.

Given enough time, Alain would add God to his list of fanciful ideas. Time enough to drink one more espresso would do. The concept of a Supreme Being, he'd say, is the greatest myth of them all. Only dreamers and young children really believe that God or anything else exists beyond the senses. Wiser, worldly, sophisticated people like him cultivate more rational worldviews. Yeah, he's scoffing at me, all right. I'm just a fugitive of reality in all my grubby, deep-woods dreaminess. As far as he's concerned, I'm just another starry-eyed fool thinly veiling my God-talk with wildness, making more of nature than I should.

Opening my eyes, I spot two unmolested food bags dangling from the trees. A smile breaks across my face as I jump out of bed. And even though he's been dead over half a century, I talk to Alain as if he's right here in camp with me.

"I can't tell you how good it makes me feel to see those two bags," I say out loud, "Now I'm home free. Now I can venture deep into this wilderness and experience something that you can't possibly understand in all your smug, urban rationalism. You're right about one thing: I'm on the run. But what I'm running towards is more important than what I've left behind. Yeah, I've been where you are. I've lounged in that café, sipping espresso, enjoying all the amenities of high civilization. But I always return to these woods, because something out here feels right to me. It's something you won't find in a city. As difficult as it might be for you to imagine, Alain, not all good things are civilized. Some of them aren't even human."

MIDMORNING. Back on the trail. The forest floor is littered with beechnuts.

I haven't seen anything like this in a long time. No wonder the squirrels are so excited. It's a bonanza for them. It's a bonanza for the other forest animals, as well. Occasionally, I step over a pile of beechnut shucks left behind by some feasting forest creature. And even more beechnuts are raining down from the trees. Why hadn't I noticed them before?

I plant my trekking poles firmly in the ground while forging ahead at a pace too strong to maintain for more than a few minutes. West Lake is seven miles ahead, and the prospect of reaching it brings a tear to my eye. I'm going to reach that magical, mystical place today, by God. My poles knock against roots and rocks as I race down the trail, humming and sobbing for joy. What a sentimental old fool I am. But it doesn't matter. I'm alone, so I can get as maudlin as I want. Just me and the other wild animals. I've been here before and am happy to be here again, driving deeper into a forest in hot pursuit of God-knows-what, anticipating salvation. I'm ten miles deep into this wilderness. Make that eleven miles. I'm a sweating, panting, hiking machine. I stop long enough to stretch, eat an energy bar, and suck down half a liter of water. Then I resume my march. Nothing can stop me now.

Just north of Spruce Lake, the trail begins a long ascent. I cut my pace. The sun shines brightly through the trees, from a sky more blue than white. After passing between two small mountains, the surrounding spruce and fir forest gives way to a stand of hardwoods. I am surprised to see so many maples already in their autumn garb—bright red and orange leaves illuminating the canopy overhead—but I'm twenty-five hundred feet above sea level right now, so this color isn't really all that early. Fall comes fast to the highlands.

Back in the spruces, I skirt rotting puncheon stretched across mud holes. Evidently, some trail maintenance crew came through here ten or fifteen years ago, doing some extensive work. But no one has done anything since. This deep into the woods, it would be a major undertaking to repair this trail. Where are the resources for it? Never enough money or manpower. It always comes back to that.

Where did the trail go? While standing before a small waterfall where Sampson Bog becomes a stream, I look around for trail markers that seem to have disappeared. Then I notice a beaten path on the far side of the waterfall. "No way," I groan in disbelief, but there's no denying the obvious. The remains of a footbridge twisted in the rocks below make it clear what has happened here. Come to think of it, I remember reading somewhere that this bridge had been washed out. So I look around and, sure enough, I find ribbons tied to trees. They mark the way down to a stream crossing. A log stretches across the stream, just below the waterfall. Not much of a bridge, but it'll do.

While using my trekking poles to balance myself on the log, I cross the stream without getting my feet wet. On the other side, I stop just long enough to enjoy sunlight dancing along the top of the waterfall. A restless torrent splashes among the jumble of rocks below it. The light-and-water show mesmerizes me. When finally I wrench myself free of its spell, I climb up the bank and tag the trail continuing northward.

Up and down and around, the trail meanders through an expansive forest. It winds through trees and across small bogs for two long miles. By the time I reach West Canada Creek, I'm ready for a break. On the other side of a wooden footbridge spanning the creek, I drop my pack. It now weighs half a ton. I bitterly recall what John Muir once said: "Only by going alone in silence, without baggage, can one truly get into the heart of the wilderness." Well, I have the "alone in silence" part down cold, but am completely overloaded with "baggage." No doubt that old mountaineer would be shaking his head if he could see me now. A fifty-pound pack, for chrissakes. I'm getting muscle spasms in my shoulders because of it. A blanket, a good knife, and a crust of bread were all that old John ever needed. True, I'm prepared for every contingency, but who's the smarter backcountry traveler? Someday I'm going to wander as he did.

A half hour later, I stop and eat lunch at the South Lake lean-to. I could easily press on to West Lake, but there's no reason to rush. South Lake is as good a place to be as any. A steady wind blows the sky clear of white, puffy clouds. Water gently laps to the sandy shore. It's a fair day with temperatures in the sixties. Good weather for daydreaming.

My boots get wet on the way to the bridge that separates South Lake from a huge wetland. There's simply not enough planking in the mud. The bridge itself is an elaborate wooden structure that can't be more than a decade old. It dwarfs the nearby beaver lodge. Yeah, the bridge is impressive, but the woodwork on either side of it seems like an afterthought. The planks between the bridge and high ground on the far shore sink several inches into the lake when I step on them. Water rushing over the planks thoroughly soaks my boots. I ponder this quirky arrangement while slipping back into the woods. The builders came close to making this a dry crossing—close, but no cigar. Oh well. I take the bridge for what it's worth. I couldn't have crossed the deep channel between the lake and the wetland without it.

I hike over one last hill, then ease down the trail towards the object of my desire. West Lake comes into full view as I approach a shelter on its shore. The unoccupied lean-to looks inviting. I drop my pack and immediately start tidying up the place to make it my own. I have arrived. There are sixteen miles of trail to the nearest road behind me, and another fifteen to the next road ahead. Talk about deep woods! It doesn't get much deeper than this. And it looks like I'm going to have the place all to myself, at least for now.

Chapter 7

THE HUGE MOUND OF ASHES in the fire pit is still warm to the touch. In fact, when I dig a few inches into it with my fingers, I nearly burn myself. Last weekend, five young men threw a party here. They were the last people to make entries in the lean-to journal. I look around. There's no indication that anyone else has been here since then. Today is Thursday. Could the remnants of their campfire have smoldered all that time? Hardly seems possible, but this much is certain: it was a big, hot fire. The ash pile is deep.

It takes nearly an hour to kill the heat. In the process, I dump enough water on the ashes to douse a bonfire. I pull trash from the fire pit and the shelter until a gallon-sized plastic bag is stuffed full. There's nothing I can do about the empty liquor bottles other than wash them out. According to the journal entries, at least one of the young men who partied here was in the military. That explains all the Meals-Ready-to-Eat condiments left behind. When I think about where that soldier has been recently—in a war zone overseas, most likely—I don't feel so bad about cleaning up after him. I collect all the liquor bottles, both empty and half-full, and place them on one of the two shelves inside the lean-to. Then I go foraging for firewood.

West Lake is the crown jewel of this wilderness to be sure. Its clear, deep water stretches westward to a distant, forested shore. I imagine a couple backcountry anglers casting from a boat in the middle of this lake, hauling a fifteen-inch brook trout out of the water. Two loons float about, occasionally calling out. There's a small, rocky island not more than a hundred yards off shore. It lends character to this place. The cluster of big boulders just north of camp looks like a good spot to cast a line. I'll have to go over there later on and try my luck. After all, the backpacker's fly rod I've been carrying with me since Benson hasn't seen action yet.

I take my time breaking up sticks and stacking them neatly next to the fire pit. Now I have enough fuel for several cooking fires. Good to get that task out of the way. Work before pleasure, always, though I must admit that I enjoy snapping and stacking firewood. Yeah, I like doing simple domestic tasks around camp. I am not immune to that all-too-human urge to make the world a more orderly place.

The sun shines brightly in late afternoon while I scribble in my journal. A strong breeze chases away the last few wispy clouds. I bask in deep forest solitude, half expecting a tired hiker or two to stumble into camp any minute now. But no one shows. Just me, the loons, a few songbirds, and a lapping lake. I write in my journal that I really should drop a line in the water soon. Then I set my pen aside. Why not now?

Down by the water's edge, I rock-hop as far out as I can go without slipping into the drink. A woodpecker flies overhead. The laughter of loons pierces the silence. The red-hot sun burns larger than life, just above the distant shore. The strong afternoon breeze fades to evening stillness. An azure sky deepens to cobalt blue directly overhead—the gateway to the universe slowly opening. I'm no longer a woodswalker. Now I'm a man alone on a lake surrounded by sprawling forest, on a planet that's teeming with life. And it feels good.

What a strange feeling it is to be here, standing on a big rock and casting a fly across still water. I'm out of touch, at least temporarily, with the rest of humanity. Out here alone like this, I feel truly free. I feel like the master of all I survey. No inhibitions. There are no social conventions here to confound me, no smooth-talking propagandists to befuddle my thoughts. Just earth, sky, water, and self. I am giddy with the prospect of unqualified freedom, yet my casting remains rhythmic, steady and resolute. Zen fly-casting. Each breath I take is an unconscious prayer, a tactile acknowledgement of something invisible yet no less real out here—something so true about the world that it must be sacred. A sharpening awareness of this electrifies me in mid-cast. So when my line settles onto the lake's surface, I tip my hat in deep reverence to the ineffable forces all around me.

A dragonfly buzzes low over the water, picking off unsuspecting midges. A few small fish—shad, I believe—feed next to the huge boulders nearby. The water's surface ripples as some unseen predator below sucks down a mayfly. I cast my line towards the ever-expanding rings it leaves behind. I work a wet fly through the water, several inches beneath the surface, until a deep tug convinces me that trout are lurking there. But nothing more happens after that. No matter. It feels good just standing here, surveying this wild world as the sun sinks into the trees and the horizon bursts into flame.

I listen to the hypnotic sound of nothing, nothing at all, until my ears ring. Then the bats come out. When at last I can no longer see my fly on the water, I stumble back towards camp though a thick stand of dark spruces. No fish fry tonight, but I've taken my fill of an elemental existence. I've taken my fill despite the fact that Nature itself remains a profound mystery to me. That's Nature with a capital "N." There is more to it than mere appearances suggest. What I learn about it during my studies and what I experience firsthand during times like this are two entirely different things. There is the natural world subdivided into its discernible particulars, and then there is Nature as a whole, defying explanation. All I can do is marvel at it.

DINNER AFTER DUSK. I build a ridiculously small fire atop the flattened mound of cold ashes in the fire pit and boil up some ramen noodles. I eat nuts and dried fruit while slurping down the noodles. Then I sling my food bags. The few thumb-sized sticks burn down to coals, giving my eyes something to focus on as my mind empties. When only a handful of embers remain, I settle into the shelter for the night. An owl hoots from somewhere in the forest as if to remind me that it's time to get some sleep. I take the suggestion to heart.

IN THE MIDDLE OF THE NIGHT, I awaken abruptly to the call of loons. They fall silent just as quickly as they called out, but I remain awake. A full moon shines brightly in the center of the sky. Its soft light reflects off the mirrored lake, pooling in my eyes. I stare at it through a glassy stupor, listening intently. Something is missing. I raise my head to listen even more intently, but still don't hear it. What am I not hearing? Can't put my finger on it. No sound of water lapping shore, no sound of crickets, frogs, or anyone else. That's it! Everything is missing. There's only absolute stillness and the deafening silence that stillness makes.

When finally I do hear something between my own deep breaths, I am surprised by it. I hear a humming noise—the sound of a pulsing motor or something like that. I've heard this sound before but it's been so long that I can't place it. The sound of civilization in the distance perhaps? Lord knows I'm too far away from the mechanized world to hear the collective sound it makes. No, that's not it. It's something else, something *organic*. And with that realization, I bolt upright in my sleeping bag. Is it me? I listen carefully while holding my breath and yes, by god, it's me. The sound of a circulatory system hums in my ear. Not just a heartbeat, the actual rush of blood, as well—the sound of a vital force coursing through my veins. Suddenly a barred owl hoots, breaking the intense silence. I clear my throat loudly, reorienting myself to a more mundane reality. Yet the moon still shines brightly through the colorless night.

Sitting up now, it's even easier for my eyes to drink in the moonlight. I lose all sense of self in the craters, mountains, and valleys visible on that celestial sphere. Time stops. Shadows, shadows—the world beneath that sphere is a dozen shades of grey in varying textures and shapes. Suddenly the vast and frigid universe beyond the moon extends towards the earth, reaching deep within me until it taps the vital force humming there. Now that force is escaping into the world and, for a split second, I feel connected to all things. Then I shiver violently, reverting back to a small bubble of existence, regaining self-consciousness.

I'd better get back to sleep, I tell myself, but that's easier said than done. Both the loons and the owls are at it now, singing dissonant yet alluring melodies while a croaking bullfrog nearby lays down a solid baseline. It's a wild symphony! But I have to get some sleep. The eastern sky is growing lighter already, so I close my eyes to block out the premature arrival of morning. I close my eyes and quickly depart this world. Next thing I know, I am wandering through the cosmos with no clear idea who I am or what's going on. Nor can I tell whether I'm dreaming or still awake. The line between self and other has blurred completely. I have become a creature of the ether.

WATER LAPS QUIETLY TO SHORE as my eyes open to daylight. My stomach is growling. I get up, stumble into the woods to pee, then kneel down by the shore's edge to splash water on my face. I search the lake for loons. A couple red-crested mallards float by. I drop my food bags and immediately start a fire.

That was one hell of a night. Not sure what it was all about. After breakfast, while sipping coffee, a stream of words pours out of my head and onto paper. A poem is born—the first one I've written in years. Trying to capture what happened last night is next to impossible. The whole affair defies understanding, as all such experiences do. Yet I scribble away all the same. Common sense never stops the poet.

Sleep and wakefulness. The world is never quite as it seems. We sleep-walk through our lives for the most part, oblivious to reality's edge, lost in the mundane. We cultivate a false sense of being in control of our lives, of understanding the world around us. But it is largely an illusion. As Annie Dillard wrote in her book, *Holy the Firm*, we are asleep at the switch most of the time. Moments of true wakefulness and clarity are rare. And when we do occasionally awaken, we are surprised by what greets us. "We wake, if we ever wake," Dillard said, "to the silence of God."

I don't pretend to understand the world around me any better than the next guy, but I have learned over the years to recognize the marvelous when I encounter it. And that's precisely what I encountered last night. I set myself up for it by coming out here, certainly. In that regard, the experience was contrived. But sometimes nothing the least bit remarkable occurs when you set yourself up, and other times you get more than you bargained for. I've learned to measure the intensity of a mystical experience by the amount of surprise it generates. Last night I was very surprised. In fact, I'm not quite sure what to make of it. Then again, I never do know what to make of such experiences.

A *mystical* experience? Yeah, I'm willing to call it that, for lack of a better word. I'd call it something extraordinary, at least. There's no good way to label such experiences. Mist, mystery, mystical—by definition such things are hazy and inexact. Occasionally the mind makes discoveries that reason cannot follow. Strictly rational creatures think this is absolute hogwash. I understand their skepticism. But you can't experience anything extraordinary if you don't first open your mind to the possibility. I wonder how many rationalists have ever spent a week alone in the wild. Mystifying experiences are not uncommon out here. The immediacy of the wild has a way of undercutting even the most rigorous systems of thought. After thirty-odd years of woods wandering, I've learned that much, anyhow.

William James said in *The Varieties of Religious Experience*: "Certain aspects of nature seem to have a peculiar power of awakening such mystical moods." I agree, though I'm not quite sure what those "mystical moods" are, where they come from, or why. In the bright light of day, with my so-called mystical experience under the magnifying glass of cold-blooded reason, I seriously question its validity. In my youth, I stepped over that boundary between sanity and madness on several occasions, so I know all too well how easy it is to delude oneself. But last night was a different matter. Last night there was only an elemental encounter, surprising in its directness and simplicity—mystical only inasmuch as it drew me out of myself for a short while. What else can I say? The more one talks about such things, the less sense they make.

Enough with all this esoteric nonsense already. It's time to get back down to earth. My hiking clothes stink. They need to be cleaned. A strong wind is blowing, so they'll dry fast when I hang them. With that in mind, I dig a hole, line it with plastic, and fill it with water. A little biodegradable soap and voila!—one backwoods washing machine. The rinse cycle is a change of water. Soon my clothes are flapping in the breeze. Then I attend to other matters: reorganizing food bags, gathering more firewood, and filtering water for drinking. I listen to nuthatches, chickadees and buzzing insects while puttering about camp. I toss a few nuts to the vole poking his head out of a crevice at the base of the fire pit. Patches of muted yellow and red foliage adorn the green hills beyond the lake. I'd snap a picture of it if I thought my camera could do the scene justice. But it can't, so I simply enjoy the view. And the rest of the morning slips away quickly.

Chapter 8

MIDDAY. I lounge amid rocks along the edge of West Lake, scribbling in my journal while taking in the view. A warm wind ripples water gleaming beneath a blazing sun. A few clouds roll in, but they're too white and puffy to pose any threat. Loons dance across the lake's surface. Mergansers float nearby. The rocky cliffs protruding from the mountain just beyond the lake beg to be climbed, but I'm too comfortable right now to seriously consider the prospect. Maybe I'll climb them the next time I come here. It's clear that my relationship with this place is just beginning.

No wonder French Louie liked it here. Woods, water, wildlife, deep forest solitude—West Lake has everything a backwoodsman could ever want. I can see why that old hermit lived next to this lake as long as he did. I'd certainly enjoy spending a few years alone in a place like this. Or would I?

In 1868, Louis Seymour left the circus and went to work for a logging outfit at Lewey Lake. He roamed this wild country with other trappers for several years before finally taking up residence here at West Lake. From that point on, he was known as French Louie—an eccentric, unwashed, yet friendly fellow who kept snakes as pets. Periodically, he would go into town to sell his furs and get drunk. But he stayed to himself for the most part, immersed in all this wild beauty. It was a good life, no doubt, for someone who could be alone for months on end. Ah, but there's the rub.

French Louie must have *loved* being alone. As for me, well, I like people too much to be without them very long. A couple weeks of deep forest solitude is all I can handle.

Speaking of which, when was the last time I saw anyone? Today is Friday. Last person I talked to was that pleasant woman behind the post office counter in Piseco. That was Tuesday—three days ago. Maybe that's why French Louie paid so little attention to calendars. The more one thinks about the passage of time, the more it becomes an issue. Better to simply be in the moment and forget the rest. Hmm…maybe I should enjoy being alone while I can. I'm sure it'll be a different story a week from now, when I'm in the High Peaks. That's a busy neck of the woods. Hikers all over the place. Even tomorrow, at Cedar Lakes, I will probably run into someone. Yeah, enjoy this solitude while I can.

TWO BACKPACKERS SUDDENLY APPEAR while I'm puttering about camp late in the afternoon. The tall, lanky fellow standing before me calls himself Hans. His much shorter female companion is Christina. From the expressions on their faces, I can tell that they had hoped to have this lean-to all to themselves. I know that feeling well. I inform them that there's another lean-to on this lake, about a half mile north. Haven't seen anyone out here for days, so it's probably unoccupied. Out of courtesy I invite them to join me, but that's not what any of us want. In fact, they don't even take off their packs while we're talking. They don't want to make even that much of a commitment to being here.

Hans and Christina are from Boston. They are hiking the Northville-Placid Trail in sections. Earlier this week, they hiked through the High Peaks Wilderness. Yesterday they left their car at Piseco and walked to Spruce Lake. Now here they are. Seasoned backpackers in their thirties, obviously in good shape, they can pretty much hike as long and as hard as they want. Yet they plan on wandering aimlessly about the West Canada Lakes Wilderness for the next two or three days. It's good to hear this. It's good to know that even among younger, more athletic people, there are those who value being in the wild more than the big brag of hiking a trail as fast as possible.

After divulging that I'm a nature writer of sorts—something that usually comes up during backwoods conversations—I ask them what they do. Hans and Christina hesitate a moment before telling me that they are biochemists. Actually, Christina works in a more administrative capacity for the company. But Hans is a bona fide scientist. They tell me this with some apprehension, no doubt expecting a barrage of probing questions. What exactly do they do? Who do they work for? Have they sold out to some sinister chemical company that's messing around with Mother Nature? Maybe yes, maybe no. I don't pry. The way I see it, everyone should be free to roam these woods without fear of being scrutinized by others. There are plenty of opportunities for that back in the lowlands. So I quickly change the subject.

I grab my camp towel and head for the water as soon as Hans and Christina leave. I need to dunk this grubby body of mine in the lake before evening comes and it's too chilly to do so. While bobbing in a fairly deep hole amid the big rocks, I wonder if anyone one else will come along today. I certainly hope not. A half hour with Hans and Christina took care of my need to socialize. Now I'm quite comfortable being alone again. So it goes. It doesn't take much to check that creeping sense of isolation.

While standing naked on a rock, toweling myself dry, I wonder if my new neighbors can see me. I doubt they can, but the possibility makes me turn my back to the woods. The distance between us seems like nothing.

EVENING EARLY. Dragonflies swoop along the shoreline. Two loons dip into the lake very close by. They are fishing, as I am. Just like yesterday, I watch the sun set slowly over the lake. But this time there's no rush to get back to camp. I've already eaten dinner and slung my food bags, so there's no reason to leave the water before darkness is complete. I fish until the bats come out, then I fish a bit longer. No trout rise. I catch only a couple of dace. Whatever. The profound silence is reason enough to stand here. Half a mile to my right, I see a plume of smoke rolling out of the woods. No doubt Hans and Christina are enjoying the quiet as much as I am.

Back at the lean-to, I waste no time getting ready for bed. It's not even eight thirty when I settle into my sleeping bag. Big day tomorrow. In fact, I have several big days ahead of me now. I have only nine days left to cover the eighty-plus miles of trail between here and Lake Placid. I'll have to get serious about making tracks in order to hike the entire NPT in the allotted time. My feet have calloused over and I'm in fairly good shape. Physically I could do it—if I press hard, that is. Or I could just hang out here a while longer. Yeah, I've been in this situation before. When I hiked the Long Trail, I reached a point where it came down to the same hard decision: gear up or gear down?

A part of me wants to get moving again. Another part of me wants to stay here at West Lake and groove with the wild until my food runs out. Tough choice. The wild is a temptress, urging me to see her as French Louie did and stop thinking in terms of time and distance. Get going or stay put? It's a pleasant conundrum, actually. Either way I win.

HOW FORTUNATE WE ARE to have large pockets of wilderness in which to roam. How remarkable that such places exist in a country like the United States, where economic growth is so important. But forest preservation doesn't happen by itself, nor is it sustained by mere whim. Such things have a way of disappearing over time. The Forest Preserve, created in 1885, would have been nibbled out of existence long before now if certain loggers, miners, and developers had had their way. But the people of New York prevented that from happening.

In 1894, the New York State Constitution was amended so that the Adirondack (and Catskill) Forest Preserve would be "forever kept as wild forest lands." The amendment specified that these lands "shall not be leased, sold or exchanged, or be taken by any corporation, public or private, nor shall the timber thereon be sold, removed or destroyed." New York voters approved this change in the general election that year, making "forever wild" more than just a pleasant-sounding phrase. That was a good day for the conservation movement. For the first time ever, anywhere in the nation, the wildness of a forest was constitutionally guaranteed.

A couple years prior to this amendment, the State of New York had established the Adirondack Park. Soon officials were drawing the boundaries of the Park on state maps with a thick blue line. That line marked the beginning of a new era. While much private land still existed inside the blue line, the Forest Preserve was expected to grow until it encompassed the better part of the Park. And so it has. Nowadays, the Adirondack Park incorporates six million acres—roughly the size of Vermont—and over half of that land is Forest Preserve. In terms of sheer size, it rivals any tract of land similarly protected out west.

Forever wild? "Forever" is a big, uncompromising word. In a nation predicated on growth, in a culture as focused on material well-being as ours, who can say with absolute certainty that the Adirondacks will always be wild? No one can. But the intention is there, anyhow.

Chapter 9

SATURDAY MORNING, seventh day in the woods. On the move again. I sign into a trail register located in the middle of a clearing just north of the lean-to. Then I head east. The trail veers away from a low spot flooded by beavers, staying on high ground while skirting Mud Lake. Refreshed from a day of rest, I make good time. I charge down the trail, well aware that a dozen miles of rough terrain stretch between where I started this morning and where I want to be tonight. No matter. I stop and take a break when the path underfoot tags the shoreline of the shallow lake. I look around while munching trail mix, hoping to see a moose. Mud Lake is an oversized version of the many bog-like ponds I've seen on this trip so far—places that are more wetland than open water. Ideal moose habitat. But none of those large herbivores step into view while I'm watching.

The trail rises abruptly from Mud Lake, drops down, crosses a stream, then rises again. I huff and puff up a short, steep incline, feeling the full weight of my backpack. Adjusting hip and shoulder straps, I distribute the load evenly across my body. But fifty pounds is still fifty pounds. I grunt and sweat, leaning hard on my trekking poles every time they hit the earth. Forward progress is painfully slow. I grumble every step of the way. Then I hear a footfall, look up, and nearly jump out of my skin.

"Hey," a young man says rather nonchalantly, appearing out of nowhere. I return the greeting. He and his female companion stop a few feet away. Their small, scruffy-looking dog comes over and sniffs my leg. With so few people on the trail this time of year, a chance encounter like this is an event. I lean on my trekking poles while politely asking them about their hike. They tell me that they came into the woods yesterday from a trailhead near Pillsbury Mountain. They are doing a three-day loop. He's a lean hiking machine, fresh from an end-to-end hike on Vermont's Long Trail. She's a novice hiker, clearly more interested in being with him than being out here. Oddly enough, neither one of them appears to be sweating. Then again, they are young and in good shape. Early twenties, I'd say. Besides, their packs are small. They live nearby, in a small town just inside the Blue Line. This sprawling wilderness is their back yard. That partly explains their casual, light-footed approach to these woods.

The young woman marvels at the sheer size of my pack. "Yeah, I'm ready for anything," I respond, adding that I'm thru-hiking this trail. The young man figures that most of my load is food. I don't tell him otherwise. But after we part ways, I feel like a fool for carrying so much stuff. Do I really need the extra clothing, two water bottles, a complete mess kit, a camp stove, and fishing paraphernalia? I should look into buying some ultra-light gear: a sleeping bag that weighs only two pounds, a rain jacket that fits in the palm of my hand—things like that. The size of my pack shouldn't impress anyone. I wish it could be mistaken for a daypack. I amble alone down the trail, berating myself for not shaving off the unnecessary pounds when I was packing for this trip. My pack is way too heavy.

Weight or no, I pick up my pace after cresting a small hill. I hum a few tunes while easing down its north slope. My trekking poles click against rocks as I swing them forward. A short water break at the southernmost end of Cedar Lakes, then I'm off and running again. I hike over Cobble

Hill so fast that the bridge between Beaver Pond and Cedar Lakes takes me by surprise. Here already? Just then I notice how familiar the surrounding landscape looks. Yeah, I've been here before.

In 2002, I hiked into West Canada Lakes Wilderness from the northeast. I had my ailing German shepherd, Jesse, with me at the time. It was her last big outing before I put her down. We made it this far west before turning due north towards Lost Pond. Then we looped back towards the trailhead, shaving miles off our trek. We camped here at Cedar Lakes for two nights. I hooked a brook trout along this shoreline and Jesse chased it away. Four years later, here I am again—this time by myself. Suddenly I miss my four-legged companion. She accompanied me on so many treks that I still look behind me when I hike, half expecting to find her there. Her ghost follows me up the trail as far as the Lost Pond trail junction. There it wanders northward while I keep to the NPT. And the next half a mile is full of sadness and longing.

I reach the lean-to at the northeastern end of Cedar Lakes in no time. I had planned on eating lunch here but the pair of backpacks dumped on the lean-to floor change my mind. I go down by the water's edge, instead. I drop my pack on the rocky beach and settle against a large stone for a long break. Two middle-aged hikers are swimming thirty yards offshore. I ignore them, looking the other direction while munching away. One of the two men comes over to me a while later. He says "Hello," then asks the usual questions. He's happy to learn that I don't intend to stay here tonight, that I'll be continuing my trek northward after lunch. I'm not rude but I'm not exactly friendly, either. Not sure what's gotten into me. Just not in the mood for idle talk, I guess. Just want to finish my lunch in peace and get back on the trail.

The weather has me worried. A strong wind has kicked up during the past half hour. Dark clouds are gathering overhead.

"Would like to stay and chat," I say to the two men a short while later as they're busy organizing their gear in the lean-to, "But I have a date with destiny!" I hope to make it five miles up the trail to the Cedar River lean-to before the heavy weather arrives. I tell them as much. They wish me luck as I walk away. I'll need it. The sky overhead looks ominous.

While distancing myself from the only shelter around for miles, I start thinking about something I read a couple weeks ago. In a book called *Luck: The Brilliant Randomness of Everyday Life*, Nicholas Rescher says luck is a rogue force that keeps our lives from being managed rationally. How true. The next shelter is a couple hours away. Will the storm catch me before I get there? Hard to say. Maybe it'll pass to the south; maybe it'll stall out. Or maybe I'll be zinged by it. There's no way to know for certain what'll happen this afternoon. So I read the sky, throw the dice, hope for the best. Considering the clouds thickening overhead, it's a risky play.

A couple hundred yards down the trail, I pass three grinning young men with fishing poles in hand. They will soon be joining the two middle-aged backpackers at the lean-to behind me, I imagine. "Where are you going?" I ask them.

"Crazy," one of them responds with a goofy laugh, convincing me that I made the right call. Yeah, keep moving, rain or no rain. Better to get soaked than to share a seven-by-ten lean-to with five mismatched strangers.

Thunder rumbles in the distance as I go deeper into the darkening forest. I race down the trail, thinking that I might be able to dodge the worst of the approaching storm if I can get far enough north. The storm sounds like it's passing mostly south of here. But rain starts falling as I crest Lamphere Ridge. Nothing I can do now but stoically accept my fate. I drop my pack and secure the rain-resistant cover over it. Next I don a cheap, vinyl poncho, expecting the worst. And the worst comes. A light rain builds to a downpour as thunder draws closer. I hunker down beneath the thick boughs of a young spruce, covering as much of my body as possible with the poncho. Water streams off my rain hat. A puddle gathers in my lap. Lightning flashes through tree limbs swaying in a fierce wind. It's a bad one. I watch the trees, waiting for them to start falling down around me. Fortunately they don't. But I cower in the spruces all the same as Mother Nature rages.

When finally the worst of the storm passes, I return to the trail and resume my hike. I'm hoping the movement will dry me out a bit. It doesn't. The torrential downpour has thoroughly soaked the forest, and the poncho I'm still wearing doesn't protect my legs from the wet vegetation brushing against them. Oh well.

NEVER HAS A SHELTER LOOKED BETTER TO ME. The Cedar River lean-to is an outpost of dryness in a vast, dripping universe. Miles of mud puddles, saturated brush, and my own sweat have finished what the downpour started. I'm completely drenched now. Ah, refuge. I sigh with relief while slipping beneath the lean-to's sturdy, watertight roof. I drop my damp pack in the corner of the shelter, away from where I intend to sleep tonight. Then I strip off my wet gear. I towel off before opening a precious bag of dry clothes. The thermal shirt that I pull from it is a tactile delight. The pants are even better. And while I'm not about to break into song, putting on these dry clothes greatly improves my mood.

Only later, once muted daylight has faded to twilight, does it occur to me that I'll have to go back out and sling a line in the trees. I was smart enough to pump two full liters of water from a stream while I was hiking, so I don't have to deal with that, but I'll still have to hang food bags later on. Dammit! I switch back into my wet hiking pants for the task, then scurry barefoot and half naked through the drizzle to a large maple behind the shelter. There I toss a line over a branch ten feet above my head. That'll do. Then quickly I return to my dry sanctuary. After I've finished munching trail mix and granola bars, I'll go back out and sling the food bags. No cooking or subsequent cleanup in the rain this evening. Keeping it simple.

A big-eared mouse pops out of a crack in the floor while I'm writing in my journal and eating. He makes a play for my food bag, now resting in the middle of the shelter floor. I bark at him halfheartedly. He's not impressed. He runs back to his hole only to reemerge a few minutes later. I toss a dirty sock at the intruder and that makes him flinch. Still he's undeterred. So I wait until he's only inches away from my food bag, then I lunge towards him with a nasty growl. That does the trick.

I sling my food bag in the last remaining glint of light, imagining a black bear leaping out of the bushes behind me. But, as the poet Theodore Roethke once said, not all bushes are bears. The task is completed without event. Then comes a real concern—one so mundane that I'm reluctant at first to acknowledge it. I'm lonely.

Loneliness hounds me all the way back to the lean-to. The forest silence, encroaching darkness, and persistent drizzle give it teeth. I've been here before. In the trackless wilds of Southeast Alaska over a decade ago, I wrestled with it. Back then I was all by myself during four straight days of rain and fog. In situations like that, even a guy who enjoys being alone can reach a point where solitude seems downright oppressive. As much as I hate to admit it, I miss the company of others when the weather gets like this.

Inside the shelter, I light a candle to push back the darkness. That helps. A handful of jelly beans also helps. I welcome the distraction of maps studied by lamplight. Mr. Mouse pops his head out of the hole in the floor and I'm almost glad to see him. Almost. I pound the floor to scare him away. Then I listen to water dripping off the shelter roof for a while. Time to call it a night. Twelve miles traveled today. More tomorrow. Better get some rest.

Chapter 10

DAYBREAK. Chilly, foggy, and damp. What a rude awakening after such a pleasant dream. Judy and I were going about our daily lives together. Nothing special happened, but the dream was vivid enough to seem real. Now I'm missing her. I've been on the trail a week now. That means homesickness is right on schedule. Oh well. I'm well rested after a long night's sleep and *physically* ready for the day's challenge, anyhow. I crawl out of bed with gathering resolve. The air is still. It'll be a nice day once the fog burns off.

Splashing sounds down by the river—is that a fish rising? With a grimace I slip into boots and pants still wet from yesterday's rain. Then I grab my rod. High grass along the path to the river dampens my thighs. Rings ripple across the quiet water while I rig up. It's a sure sign that fish are feeding just below the surface. I cast towards the rings once, twice, several more times, anticipating a strike. Suddenly I remember doing this exact same thing in this exact same place four years ago. Then I laugh at myself. Fooled again. The fish are feeding, no doubt, but I won't be catching them. They're too cagey for me. A beaver swims along the opposite bank, remarkably indifferent to my presence. I watch him swim about for quite some time before quitting the stream.

A bowl of cold raisin bran doesn't pack a lot of calories, but it gets me going in the morning. I chase it with a granola bar and hot coffee while reorganizing my gear. My cheap vinyl poncho has a tear in it and my favorite pair of socks is still damp. Everything I wore yesterday is still damp, except the hiking pants I'm wearing. Body heat has dried them out for the most part during the past hour. I pull on a fresh t-shirt and then pack up. By nine I'm ready to go.

A great blue heron flies low overhead—Mother Nature's air show. I hear another one calling in the distance, in the general direction of Cedar River Flow. I'm sure there are plenty of herons fishing in the reeds over there. They'll make good company when I reach that waterway later on. Thought I heard coyotes last night but it could've been herons. After all, I was half asleep and not really paying attention. Herons, beavers, coyotes—the more wildlife I encounter out here, the better. Wild encounters change the way I see things. Watching wildlife reminds me that my kind isn't the center of the universe. And for a moment, however fleeting and unexpected, I feel blessed to be in the presence of a creature that's nothing like myself.

THE HOT SPOTS ON MY FEET ache as I amble slowly down the trail. I rolled my ankles a few times yesterday and now sense a little pain there, too. Other than that, I'm good to go, feeling strong and full of energy. The sky is overcast but threatens no rain. The air temperature is climbing fast. The trail underfoot turns into a woods road on the other side of a small wetland. Walking it is easy now. The blue nodes of closed gentian dapple the grassy clearings that crop up along the way. Even the dense stands of dark conifers seem inviting this morning. It's probably just a reflection of my mood, which is steadily improving with the day.

First stop comes less than hour after leaving the lean-to. I drop my pack at a well-worn campsite on the shoreline of Cedar River Flow. I remember my sojourn here four years ago as if it was last week. The water looks much the same, full of shimmering light like any lake of comparable size. Cedar River Flow isn't a lake, though. It's just a shallow reservoir backed up behind Wakely Dam. But open water is open water as far as the loons and herons are concerned. They don't discriminate. They search for food with avian intensity, as always. I munch an energy bar and gulp down water while watching them. Then I resume my hike.

The trail is wide enough for a jeep by the time I reach the gate that keeps vehicles at bay. Goodbye West Canada Lakes Wilderness, hello Moose River Recreation Area. On the other side of the gate, I step onto a two-lane dirt road. I follow a set of deer tracks pressed deep into the sandy shoulder of the road, slowly making my way toward Wakely Dam. Two men in an old pickup truck drive past. They're wearing hunting garb. No doubt they're thinking about hoofed creatures. Deer hunting season is only a few weeks away, and they're probably looking for signs of their quarry. I wonder if they've noticed the hoof prints that I'm following. Probably not.

Even though the walk to Wakely Dam is an easy stroll, I'm a bit saddened by it. Already I'm missing the wet, gnarly path left behind and the wild country through which it passes. I'll be back, I keep telling myself, but that doesn't help much. The wilderness recedes; developed lands approach. I'm out of my element now.

It's not just the sheer size of the West Canada Lakes Wilderness that's so appealing. There's something else about the place that keeps me coming back. It has a curious mix of lakes and wetlands, plenty of deep woods quiet, and unrepentant wildness—all this and more. "Each place has its own mind, its own psyche," David Abram says in his book, *The Spell of the Sensuous*. Although the Lake Champlain Valley is all that separates New York's High Peaks from Vermont's Green Mountains, those two landscapes are worlds apart. They are as different from each other as

Alaska is from the Canadian Rockies. Every landscape has a unique character. Each elicits a particular mood. And West Canada Lakes feels to me like a place where I could die happy. I don't know why. All I do know is that a few minutes out of the wilderness, I just want to get back to it as soon as possible.

A LARGE SIGN TOUTS WAKELY DAM as the last outpost of civilization, which seems rather strange to me since I'm approaching it from its wilder side. The bold-lettered notices plastered all over the checkpoint cue motorists to the dangers of backcountry travel. Among these warning signs, there's a photo of a forty-five-year-old man who went missing in these parts several weeks ago. The remains of his camp were found a few miles down the road. I log into the vehicle register even though I have no car. You never know. Every once in a while, the wild grabs hold of a pilgrim and doesn't let go. So I leave proof that I passed through here, just in case.

I drift across the nearly empty campground towards the dam where half a dozen cars are parked. After checking out the dam, I approach a family of four getting ready for a canoe trip. I tell them I'm a thru-hiker then ask if they'd be willing to take a bag of trash off my hands. It's hermetically sealed so it doesn't stink. No problem, the forty-ish fellow says. He takes the bag from me and stashes it in his car while his wife engages me in light conversation. Their pre-teen children stare at me. Evidently, the kids have never seen anything quite like me before. Is it the pack, the way I'm dressed, or my demeanor that's so alien to them? They must live in a big city.

While several groups of day-trippers load and offload canoes and kayaks from their cars, I lounge in the grass. I munch a little trail mix while patching the hot spots on my feet. Then I put on a pair of thick, dry socks. The six-mile road walk ahead could do a number on me. My goal today is to reach the Stephens Pond lean-to by dusk without getting a new blister or opening up an old one. This patchwork should ensure that.

MIDDAY. I hike fast along Cedar River Road, past Wakely Pond and the impressive cliffs of Water Barrel Mountain, enjoying the smooth, dry surface beneath my feet. The compressed dirt and gravel surface isn't too hard. The trekking poles in my hands are good for keeping a steady rhythm while I hum a few songs. Otherwise they serve no purpose. Clouds overhead give way to blue sky. Air temperatures climb into the high sixties. What a difference a day makes! This time yesterday I was hunkered down in a thunderstorm. Now I'm basking in warmth as the sun winks at me through the trees. I'm sweating just enough to feel alive. And the miles are just melting away.

No doubt about it, this roadwalk is a cinch compared to a twisting, muddy trail littered with rocks and exposed roots. But the "No Trespassing" signs along the road are getting to me. They just won't stop. For miles and miles they hound me, threatening legal action if I step into the forest. Precious property rights. The hunting club that owns the land on either side of the road makes it clear that all these trees, rocks, ridges, and ravines belong to them. No hunting, trapping, or fishing allowed. Every hundred feet or so, there's another sign, another warning. No trespassing for any reason whatsoever. The forest around me might look like the wilderness I just left, but it's not. This land is all bought and paid for. And if I as much as take a leak on it, I'm violating someone's rights. So it goes here in America, where everything has its price. I can't wait to get back into wild country. The occasional passing truck or car I can deal with, but these signs are driving me crazy.

What about wild country? Doesn't someone own that, as well? Here in the Adirondacks, over half the land is under state control. In most other wild places the federal government calls the shots. In theory, national forests, national parks and wilderness areas belong to the people of the United States, but no one is fooled by that idealistic claim. The government still controls their use—and that's what ownership is all about. Occasionally, a non-profit organization like The Nature Conservancy will hold title to a parcel of undeveloped land, but make no mistake about it: all land is owned by *someone*. Public or private, every square inch is accounted for. So what is wilderness then? Is it nothing more than a parcel of land taken out of the real estate pool? I ponder this matter while running a gauntlet of those signs. And while these thoughts don't ruin the day, they definitely put a damper on my road-walking euphoria.

When at last I reach a turnout in the road, I stop to eat lunch. The turnout is huge—big enough to accommodate dozens of vehicles. A sign tacked to a nearby tree reveals the purpose of this turnout. This is as far as the snowplows go. From here back to Wakely Dam and beyond, the road is closed to cars and trucks during the winter, making it a snowmobile trail. That means this parking lot must be open to public use. I drop my pack next to a tree along the edge of the turnout, and then pull out my food and water. I also pull out a bag of clothes still wet from yesterday's rain. I plant my trekking poles five yards apart and string a line between them. While I'm lounging in the shade eating lunch, the clothes slung over that line will dry in the sun. A few motorists stare at the oddity as they drive past, but the makeshift clothesline works remarkably well. A long afternoon hour slips away before I pack up and start hiking again. By then everything's dry.

Back on the move, I walk the last mile and a half of road. Now the surface is paved and the "No Trespassing" forest gives way to houses and open fields. I nod towards a woman puttering in her yard. I wave to a man working on his roof. The surrounding landscape is all very civilized and genteel. Pleasant enough to pass through, certainly, but I'm aching to get back in the woods. Only one obstacle remains: McCane's Resort.

The Northville-Placid Trail passes through what used to be McCane's Resort. Once hikers were welcome here. If fact, this used to be a place where they could bunk for the night. But now this property is in the hands of a gentleman who doesn't like having hordes of hikers on his land. Consequently, this section of the trail has been officially closed to day hikers. The occasional thru-hiker like me is still allowed to cross the property, but that can't last. Eventually, the owner will bar even that. Eventually, the DEC and/or the Adirondack Mountain Club will have to reroute the NPT around McCane's. In the meantime, I gingerly step past the "No Trespassing" and "Police Take Notice" signs and head across the land in full view. Before starting my trek, I called the owner and got permission to cross his property, just as my guidebook recommended. I hope he remembers me.

I don't like walking between the house and the garage, but there's no other way to reach the woods. The rest of the land is fenced. There's a guy working in the garage. I go up to him and say hello. Assuming that he's the owner, I tell him I'm thru-hiking the Northville-Placid Trail. I called a month ago—does he remember? As the man quietly goes about his work, he informs me that he's a caretaker, not the owner. I tell him that I spoke with the owner and got permission, but he doesn't seem to care. He's too busy working. When he finally looks up and makes eye contact, he says: "You're a brave fellow."

"I am?"

"It's gonna get cold tonight."

"How cold?"

"Into the thirties," the caretaker says. The he adds with a mischievous grin: "I'll be inside where it's warm, drinkin' beer and thinkin' about you."

"Ouch!" I say while walking away, "Did you have to say that?" His laughter follows me all the way to the edge of the woods.

Ah, the forest. At first the path is a heavily rutted woods road, but soon it narrows to an ATV trail. Then NPT markers appear. After a quarter hour of hiking hard, I reach a sign marking the boundary of the Forest Preserve. I let out a sigh of relief. A quick break for water and trail mix, then I enter the Blue Ridge Wilderness Area. Free at last!

"OF WHAT AVAIL ARE FORTY FREEDOMS without a blank spot on the map?' the conservationist Aldo Leopold wrote back in 1945. Good question. Sometimes, when I am feeling overwhelmed by all the rules and regulations of our allegedly free society, I wonder the same thing. No doubt other Americans have been thinking along similar lines ever since the last vestiges of the Wild West disappeared. Constitutionally guaranteed freedoms ring hollow when someone's always breathing down your neck, telling you what you can and cannot do. Guys like me often pine for the kind of freedom that only wide open country can provide. Unfortunately, it rarely exists anymore. Oh sure, there's Alaska, but that's too far away to be of any practical use to those of us living in the Lower 48. Yeah, Alaska's a great place to visit—I can vouch for that—but what can we do on a more regular basis? We can head for the nearest pocket of wilderness to stretch our legs and be free again, if only for a short while.

Chapter 11

FOR YEARS I HIKED through protected wilderness areas without giving much thought as to how they came to be. This is only natural, I suppose. It's easy to assume that things have always been the way they are. But there were no designated wilderness areas when the first Europeans landed on this continent, when only Native Americans lived here. In fact, there were no such places during the first few hundred years of Euro-American settlement. The very idea of wilderness, as we now perceive it, is relatively new. It was born in the minds of those who love all things wild and free, shortly after these things started disappearing. It arose from a longing for something authentic, unmanufactured, just as the Industrial Revolution was kicking into high gear. Oddly enough, this idea of wilderness emerged as we were becoming more civilized, as the wild within us became harder to find. In a sense, it reflects a desire to preserve that which we have taken for granted for thousands of years: an essential link to the earth itself.

In 1918, when two teenage boys named Bob and George Marshall climbed their first Adirondack peak, Whiteface Mountain, no one could have guessed that they would soon rise to prominence in the fledgling wilderness movement. Their father had hired a local woodsman, Herbert Clark, to guide them up the mountain. Evidently, Clark did his job well. The hike triggered an overwhelming passion for wild uplands in the hearts of both Marshall brothers. During the five years that followed, they hiked up forty-two other Adirondack peaks, all reaching more than four thousand feet above sea level. By 1925, they had climbed four more peaks, each exactly four thousand feet high, thus becoming the first people to ascend the forty-six "high peaks" of the Adirondacks. The "Forty-Sixer" club came into existence shortly thereafter, consisting of those who have walked in their footsteps, literally. But more importantly, two tireless champions for wilderness preservation emerged. And soon they were leaving their mark on the world in a major way.

Bob Marshall went on to work for the U.S. Forest Service as a young man, and acquired a PhD in Forestry from Johns Hopkins University at about the same time. His father, Louis Marshall, was a lawyer who had played a critical role developing the language in the 1894 amendment to the New York constitution that kept the Forest Preserve "forever wild." Bob carried on the fight for preservation while he was at the Forest Service, quickly becoming one of its most energetic and outspoken advocates. In 1935, he founded the Wilderness Society along with his brother George, the renowned naturalist Aldo Leopold, and a half dozen other conservationists. Their dedication to the cause went beyond mere words. In the early years of the Society, Bob was its principle financial backer. And when he passed away, his brother took his place.

The Wilderness Society is still in existence today. It's a non-profit organization dedicated to protecting the wildness of publicly held lands in the United States: national forests, wildlife refuges, national parks, and the like. From the word go, its members lobbied for the creation of wilderness preserves. Unfortunately, Bob Marshall died from heart disease in the late 1930s, before any of those efforts took root.

In 1945, however, a mild-mannered fellow named Howard Zahniser took up the fight. He gave up a cushy job in the U.S. Department of the

Interior to become the executive secretary of the Wilderness Society. Zahniser made things happen. Like Bob Marshall, he was a tireless advocate for wilderness protection. He worked nearly two decades for the cause—writing, speaking, and lobbying. He helped create the bill that called for a National Wilderness Preservation System, which defined wilderness areas and officially protected them. This bill first went before the U.S. Congress in the 1950s. In 1964, only months after Zahniser's death, his efforts finally came to fruition. That year President Lyndon B. Johnson signed the Wilderness Act into law.

Over the years, people like Howard Zahniser have made it clear that they value wilderness more for its intangible benefits than its recreational uses. In a speech given to the New York State Conservation Council in 1957, Zahniser asserted that we are all creatures of the wild and that by protecting it we are protecting a part of ourselves. He argued that in maintaining wilderness, "We are not, as some have thought, escaping from life but rather are keeping ourselves in touch with our true reality, the fundamental reality of the universe of which we are a part." That's a surprisingly philosophical statement for a bureaucrat-turned-lobbyist to make, no doubt. But it just goes to show how much Zahniser and those like him believed in the power of wild encounters to change people's lives. Who would have thought that such ideas were even possible in a country ruled by the almighty dollar? Perhaps there is more to being American than accounting ledgers reveal.

Nowadays, whenever I step into a pocket of wild country, I utter a little prayer of thanks. More often than not, I get my dose of the wild in places that are not designated as such. I usually tramp through national and state forests, across conservation land, or large tracts of open country owned by lumber companies. But designated wilderness areas are the only places I can count on to remain wild indefinitely. Everything else can be bought, sold, posted, altered, or developed. "Forever wild" might be too tall an order. After all, nothing lasts forever. But I believe that designated wilderness areas will still be around long after I'm dead and gone. They will remain wild for my grandchildren and their grandchildren—for as long as any of us can see into the future. That's the principle behind them, anyhow. And thank God for it!

I REACH A POINT during my late afternoon tramp into the Blue Ridge Wilderness that I decide the hike isn't as pleasant as I thought it would be. For one thing, I'm tired from the twelve miles I've already hiked today and just want to reach the Stephens Pond lean-to as soon as possible. But it's still a mile and a half away. Making matters worse, there's a big obstacle ahead. I did a little research on the Internet before starting this trip and found out that the footbridge over the wetlands just ahead is washed out. Now I'm worried. Will I be able to get across that wetland some other way? Will I have to go around it? Looking at my map, I'm daunted by the prospect. The wetland is a big one.

To my pleasant surprise, the fifteen-foot bridge spanning the channel in the middle of the wetland is right where it should be, although it leans downstream at a precarious angle, suggesting that it won't stay in place much longer. I carefully cross the tilting structure, glad that it's still here despite reports to the contrary. My boots get wet right before I step onto the bridge, but I don't care. I can't find the bottom of the narrow channel while probing its depths with a trekking pole. That only underscores my good fortune. Lady luck is my mistress now. The odds of completing this trek just changed in my favor. After two strong hiking days, I'm over halfway now. A couple more breaks like this and I'm sure to make it all the way to Lake Placid.

Long shadows consume the forest as the sun gradually sinks in the west. I push hard the last mile, leaning heavily on my trekking poles while dodging mud holes. I try to ignore the mounting pain in my shoulders, back, legs, and feet. My ankles aren't happy and my knees are starting to complain. When finally I spot the lean-to at Stephens Pond, I exhale a sigh of relief. I jettison the heavy backpack as soon as my butt lands on the lean-to floor.

Once again, I have a shelter all to myself. This is the seventh time in a row. How odd. I attribute this unlikely turn of events to the utter lack of people out here and the luck of the draw. Although a little shelter company wouldn't be a bad thing now, I'm happy to have the place all to myself. I'm getting used to spreading out. I sling a line in the trees for my food bag, then immediately go foraging for firewood. I'm too tired to mess around with a campfire this evening, but the small pile of wood will come in handy tomorrow. If what that caretaker back at McCane's says is true, I'll be glad to have a fire when I get out of bed tomorrow morning.

After collecting enough wood for two fires, I cover the pile with my poncho, and head down to the pond to fetch water. The clearing down by water's edge looks like a great place to camp. I'm tempted to drag all my things down here but, no, that'd be too much work. It's sundown already and I just want to eat and go to bed. Hmm…yet another reminder that long-distance hiking isn't the best way to experience the wild. Whatever. I enjoy watching a pair of loons dance across Stephens Pond while filling my water bottles. What's that ridge to the north of the pond? Is that Blue Mountain? I'm seeing it at an odd angle if that's the case. The ridge looks quite beautiful, reflected in placid waters that also mirror a mostly blue sky. God, how I love it out here!

The temperature drops fast as daylight fades. By sundown I'm wearing a sweater. After dinner and cleanup, I settle into my sleeping bag to study maps and make a journal entry by lamplight. Mosquitoes buzz around my head even as I don more clothes to stay warm. Mosquitoes *and* a deep chill—how is this possible? By nine o'clock, I can see my breath. I'm on my back and wandering into the land of dreams shortly after that. A loon calls out while I drift away, as if to remind me where I am. It's an Adirondack lullaby.

A CHILLY DAWN. I don't want to get out of bed. My sleeping bag is nice and warm. I rise under protest. No frost, but the air is cold enough to make getting dressed an ordeal. I waste no time starting a fire. I huddle next to it while boiling a pot of water for coffee. Robins keep me company. There are lots of them around here, along with blue jays, nuthatches, and woodpeckers. In fact, this place is thick with songbirds for some reason. And in this setting, the robins seem particularly wild and beautiful. How odd. Usually, I take them for granted. How much of what we see is a matter of context? When I'm home and going about my daily affairs, I rarely take the time to watch the robins cavorting about, searching for worms in my front yard. But out here it's a different matter. Out here it's hard to ignore them.

When I go down to the water's edge to fetch water, I am delighted by the sun's warmth. That small yellow orb burns brightly just above the trees despite a thick, cool mist still clinging to the pond. There's not a cloud overhead. It's the beginning of a beautiful day.

The campfire slows me down a bit. I go for a second cup of coffee while listening to the birds and watching them flit about, wishing I'd brought my binoculars. I take my time stretching out stiff, aching muscles. I douse the fire while packing up slowly. Even after the campfire is stone cold, I'm reluctant to leave. Only when all my things are packed and I've gone through all my maps twice do I grab my trekking poles and walk away. Add Stephens Pond to my list of places to visit again.

THE SIGNS AT THE TRAIL JUNCTION half a mile northwest of Stephens Pond are something of a wakeup call. One in particular really gets my attention: Long Lake, twenty miles. That's where my next parcel is waiting for me. I still have plenty of food—enough to keep me going for three or four days—but twenty miles seems like a great distance right now. I remind myself that I just hiked twenty-five miles in two days, but that's hardly a consolation. All of a sudden, I'm in for the long haul. Long Lake is twenty miles away and Lake Placid is another thirty-five miles beyond that. Ugh.

The path from the trail junction to Lake Durant is downhill all the way. It's a good path for daydreaming. Halfway down it, I bump into a pair of hikers heading uphill to Stephens Pond. We stop and chat, which gives them a chance to catch their breath and me the pleasure of human contact. Barbara and Steve are their names. They are spending a week in a cabin on Blue Mountain Lake and have come out for the day. They have a son who has recently hiked the Appalachian Trail so they know a few things about the thru-hiking subculture. Consequently, the questions they ask seem out of character. How long have I been out here? Where will I supply? How are my knees holding up? Talking to them is much like talking to another thru-hiker. I end up telling this pair of day hikers a lot more about myself than I normally would. I blab on and on about my hiking adventures, both past and present, until finally I catch myself. Their eyes have glazed over. I look directly at Steve and say: "Nice hat." Steve is wearing a felt hat that looks a bit out of place in the woods. I get the impression that their hike today was impromptu. Probably Barbara's idea. It's time to show mercy, regardless whose idea it was. I wish them a pleasant day and let them go.

The trail grows wider and more heavily trodden as I approach Lake Durant Campground. Next thing I know, I'm in the campground and headed the wrong way. I curse the campground maintenance crews under my breath, angry about the utter lack of signs or markers here. Then the bridge mentioned in my guidebook suddenly appears. Back on track. I wave to an elderly lady sitting in a lawn chair in front of an RV, but amble past two young fishermen without acknowledging them. Then I'm on a narrow path cutting through a small meadow. Blue Mountain looms above the trees, directly ahead. It's just as big and as beautiful as I thought it would be—the biggest mountain in this neck of the woods, reaching high into the cloudless sky like a great altar to the gods. I can hear the nearby highway traffic loud and clear. Blue Ridge Wilderness is behind me now, and my first highway crossing since Piseco is only a minute or two away.

Chapter 12

I CROSS ROUTE 30 like a wild animal, more interested in getting safely into the woods on the other side than looking around. I take note of the three cars parked at the trailhead, though. And when I sign into the trail register, I check to see who's on the trail ahead of me. Two hikers are on their way to Long Lake and back. They signed in yesterday. Since one of the cars belongs to that couple I met earlier going to Stephens Pond, I figure there must be third party somewhere on the trail who failed to register. Maybe I'll run into them, maybe I won't.

The trail into Blue Mountain Wild Forest starts easy enough, meandering over gentle ground. Then it drops into a wetland—yet another wetland. Looking at my map, I'm surprised to find that this one actually has a name: O'Neil Flow. Some nice-looking boardwalk spans a small patch of boggy ground, but the boards sink into murky water when I step on them. Oh well. I hop to high ground, shaking my head. High water in a wet year. That explains away the inadequacies of the trail work. And it's true to some extent, no doubt. But just once I'd like to hike a whole day without soaking my feet.

Suddenly the trail becomes high and dry as it wraps around the base of Blue Mountain. The ease of it, along with the balmy air and shafts of sunlight breaking through the shady forest, sets my thoughts adrift. I muse about similar places on other hikes until the past and the present blur together. As a woodswalker, I often visit this dreamy realm. It's a land populated by chipmunks and squirrels, adorned by jewelweed, tall meadow rue, and other wildflowers, where ovenbirds sing all day long. It's a place where one can still entertain romantic notions about nature. In this infinitely green landscape where ferns, witch hazel, and club moss carpet the forest floor as far as the eye can see, wildness thrives. I breathe in the subtle, exquisite mix of aromas: something sweet, the intoxicating smell of dried pine needles, rotting wood, and the earth itself. Then I see the camouflaged serpent. Whoa! Almost stepped on it! The terrified garter snake slithers into the brush while I skip forward. That snaps me out of my midday reverie.

A small stream tumbles down the mountain. The trail hugs the watery crease in the land a short while before crossing it and continuing north. This is a good place to take a break, so I settle down next to the stream for an early afternoon repast. I pump a liter of icy water and gulp down the better part of it while looking around. Murmuring brook in a calm, quiet forest. Endless green. Moss on the rocks, a cluster of mushrooms nearby, downed trees. The patches of orange and yellow in the canopy overhead reminds me what time of year it is. I wipe the sweat from my face but the dampness in my t-shirt persists. No matter. I'm comfortable out here. I'm comfortable in a way that has nothing to do with the amenities one takes for granted in civilized places. Deep within I feel the same calm that permeates the surrounding forest. I belong here. This is my home.

Enough daydreaming already. I'm going only eight miles today, but at this rate I won't reach the next shelter before dark. I shoulder my pack and get back on the trail. Push hard for a couple miles, then take it easy. Once I reach Tirrell Pond, I can lounge about and daydream all I want. But first an hour of strong hiking.

BEFORE COMMENCING THIS TREK, I learned from a website that the shelter located at the southern end of Tirrel Pond burned down not long ago, so I'll stay in the one at the northern end tonight. Despite this plan, I detour down a side trail to the southern end of the pond, thinking it might be a good place to fish. Why not? I have the time. But shortly after crossing a narrow footbridge over the pond's outlet stream, I am taken by surprise. The lean-to is still standing despite Internet reports. More importantly, there's a guy here. He looks up from his journal as I approach.

"Uh, hello," I say. The reclining fellow returns the greeting. An awkward silence follows as we both adjust to the sudden presence of someone else. Then I tell him that I'm only scouting this end of the pond for a place to fish before hiking to the shelter at the other end of the pond. He says I'll have company over there. A bunch of fishermen are camped at that lean-to. Some guide company is operating out of it right now and their clients are fishing from canoes on the far side of the pond. Hmm. This isn't what I want to hear.

When the reclining fellow asks where I started my trip, I tell him that I'm thru-hiking the NPT from Benson to Lake Placid. He's doing the same, curiously enough, but headed the opposite direction. Or at least he was until he misplaced his wallet. He had planned on provisioning at Long Lake, but without money to do so, he was forced to call his son and ask to be picked up tomorrow at Route 30. The wallet surfaced amid his gear a short while ago. Unfortunately, his son is on his way now, and there's no way to stop him. Oh well. "I'll just have to finish the trail next year," the hiker says with a heavy sigh.

"It'll still be here," I say as if that's any consolation.

"Yeah, I guess so," he responds. Then the conversation shifts to more pleasant matters: the high ridge just north of here, the stunning beauty of Cold River only a day or two beyond that ridge, and the surprising lack of people in the woods this time of year. We agree that it's like an alarm went off over Labor Day weekend, clearing the forest of hikers. So far, I've only seen a dozen people on the trail. He hasn't encountered many more than that. Did he pass a thru-hiker and his dog? Yes, in fact, he did. "The guy had his head down as if lost in thought and was hiking hard and fast. Had to say 'hello' to keep from scaring him." And on and on like that we talk until finally the fellow says: "You want a cup of coffee?'

Yes, I would. But when he pulls out a bag of freeze-dried coffee, I drop my pack and quickly dig out my own stash, thinking he'd appreciate having some fresh brew. I pour a little of my black gold into a filter while he fires up his stove. Only then do we exchange names. Only then do I ask him if he'd mind having company tonight. He insists upon it. Considering the crowd at the opposite end of the lake, he can't with good conscience send me packing.

His real name is Terry but he calls himself Limps-a-Little whenever he's on the trail. I've run into this before. A lot of long-distance hikers have trail names. A trail name keeps a hiker's wild persona separate from his or her tame one back in the lowlands. Limps-a-Little shows me the formidable knee brace that has gotten him this far. He's about my age, but unlike me he's lean and grizzled. The hard physical labor he does for work back home, the many miles of trail pounding, and the sheer passage of time have taken their toll on his body. His girlfriend didn't like the idea of him coming out here and hiking this trail by himself. What if he blows out a knee and no one's around to help him? She said his name will be Limps-a-Lot by the time he finishes the trail. "Yeah, the joints are always an issue, aren't they?" I say. We both know all about that. But there are ways around bum knees. Trekking poles can make a big difference. So can pacing oneself. Limps says that hiking slow is better than hiking fast. I concur. After all, what's the point of being out here? It doesn't make any sense to race through the woods. There's really no better place to be.

Gesturing towards the lake, Limps-a-Little says that the people on the other side of the lake have paid good money to be out here. Earlier this afternoon, he saw a float plane drop off a couple more of them. That plane is how all their camping gear and canoes got here, too. Limps doesn't like the noisy intrusion of that plane, but he recognizes the value of being out here any way one can swing it. That's why he's self-employed as a carpenter and handyman. He wants to be able to drop everything and head for the hills whenever the urge strikes. Most people can't do that. They work their tails off making money, but to what end—the occasional outing? "When they get around to dyin'," he says prophetically, "they'll find out whether it was worth it or not." Limps is betting that the endless acquisition of wealth isn't the key to a happy death. He thinks getting out here on a regular basis is far more important.

For the most part I agree with Limps' assessment, but I don't share his dislike for float planes and the noise they make. "This is a Wild Forest not a Wilderness Area," I say, "Float planes are allowed here. So are snowmobiles, I think." Then I add that everyone should have access to the wild, one way or another. Limps doesn't contest this, but he's afraid that easy access will mean a lot less deep woods solitude for guys like him and me in the long run. I make a case for the "multiple use" land policy. Limps listens politely. "Something for everyone," I finish, "And when we're old and feeble, maybe we'll be able to access the wild by wheelchair. That is, if comes to that." Limps ponders this while sipping his coffee.

In 1971, the New York State Legislature created the Adirondack Park Agency to further protect the Forest Preserve and oversee all plans for development, both public and private, within the Blue Line boundary of the park. By then the Adirondack Park had expanded to nearly six million acres, making it the largest publicly protected area in the United States, Alaska notwithstanding. Six million acres is about nine thousand square miles. That's roughly the size of Vermont. That's a big chunk of land. Too big, some would say, to be left unregulated as long as it was.

As early as 1918, the state legislature amended the constitution so that strips of the Forest Preserve could be relinquished for the construction of state highways. During the decades that followed, more highways were built and the constitution was amended several more times. In 1932, a parcel of supposedly preserved land on Mt. Hovenberg was turned into a bobsled run for the Winter Olympics in Lake Placid. In 1941, another piece of the Forest Preserve was yielded to ski trail development on Whiteface Mountain. This happened again in the late 1940s at Gore Mountain and elsewhere. In 1950, a great windstorm blew down trees on four hundred thousand acres of Adirondack land—much of it in the Forest Preserve. Logging companies were allowed to go in and salvage the downed timber so it wouldn't go to waste, thus stretching the idea of wilderness to its limit. Some say beyond. In 1959, three hundred acres of Forest Preserve were given over to the construction of Interstate 87—a move that purists argued would ruin the Park. Dozens of boundary adjustments like this occurred during the first two-thirds of the twentieth century. That's a lot of change to a landscape that has supposedly been left alone.

Considering all these changes, it's no surprise that the state legislature saw a need to devise some kind of long-term plan for the Park. Otherwise, that laudable phrase, "forever wild," would come to mean nothing. When the governor's brother, Laurance Rockefeller, issued a report in 1967 suggesting that the Adirondacks be handed over to the federal government and turned into a National Park, well, that was the last straw. No one in New York liked that idea, so the following year, a governor's commission devised a Master Plan, which the Adirondack Park Agency (APA) would later implement. That plan divided the Forest Preserve into several categories: Wilderness, Wild Forest, and Primitive Areas—each with its own set of land use regulations. Keeping things wild, it turns out, isn't as easy as it sounds.

Over a million acres of the Adirondack Park were designated Wilderness. This is one of the largest concentrations of wilderness areas in the nation, accounting for over half of all designated wilderness east of the Mississippi. No motorized vehicles are allowed in a wilderness area. There can be no roads cut into them, either, nor any permanent structures other than lean-tos. Almost as much Forest Preserve land was designated Wild Forest, accessible by float plane and snowmobiles. The remaining Primitive Areas and other so-called Intensive Use Areas are more relaxed designations, allowing a much wider array of activities. All this makes the Adirondacks a prime example of "multiple use" policy, where public lands are managed to benefit as many people as possible. But not everyone likes the APA and its regulatory ways.

Along with the implementation of the Master Plan, the Adirondack Park Agency oversees a Land Use and Development Plan that determines what can and cannot be done with all *privately* held lands within park boundaries. This frustrates many of the 130,000 people permanently residing inside the Blue Line, especially those whose livelihood depends upon steady economic growth. For all practical purposes, a park-wide zoning plan is in effect. It is designed to limit new construction to already developed areas and maintain the wildness of the Park overall. But all one has to do is look at a map showing the distribution of public and private lands in the Adirondacks and the incredible challenge here becomes obvious. The Adirondack Park is an intricate patchwork of state-held Forest Preserve lands, small towns, farms, summer homes, private clubs, resorts, and what's left of nineteenth century mining and timber ventures. It's enough to make one's head spin.

I'm all in favor of multiple use policies, both state and federal. By definition, public lands are for everyone, and "multiple use" is the only equitable way to go. But the development and implementation of those policies is tricky business, indeed. How much easier it is to be a preservationist calling for the protection of more wildlands, a developer out to make millions, or a property-rights advocate, than an APA official trying to put the Master Plan into practice. It's certainly not a job I would take on. How much easier it is to be out here in deep woods, experiencing wildness firsthand, than it is to weigh the value of wilderness against all other considerations.

If I'm reluctant to carry a banner for the endless expansion of wilderness areas, it's because I know how few woodswalkers like me inhabit this world. There isn't but one in twenty people who can use a map and compass, carry a full pack over dozens of miles of rugged trail, and fend for themselves in the wild. Factor in those who have absolutely no desire to do so and the number becomes even smaller. No, wilderness isn't for everyone. But if the average guy on the street understood the essential link between what is wild and what is human, a good portion of existing wildlands would remain forever wild no matter what. Do the APA's regulatory ways serve this end or not? That's the big question here, certainly.

Chapter 13

THE INCESSANT PROPELLER WHINE grows louder as an unseen plane approaches. Just as we're looking up, a float plane passes a few hundred feet above the trees, circles around, then lands in the middle of Tirrell Pond. Slowly it taxis towards the spit of land where canoeists had been fishing earlier. Then it disappears behind the trees. Water laps quietly to shore afterward. The blue sky is not altered by the intrusion. The mountain on the far side of the pond, sporting a bare-rock scar on its shoulder, remains unmoved. I turn to my new friend to explain how the sudden appearance of float planes kept me from feeling lonely when I was in the Alaskan bush many years ago, but Limps-a-Little is lost in his own thoughts.

"I have a hard time explaining to my girlfriend why I have to go for long hikes by myself," he says, adding that nearly everyone back home thinks he's crazy for doing so. "I hiked the Finger Lakes Trail after my divorce. It helped me work through some things. Thought I had everything worked out, but here I am again."

Limps' musings sound like a confession. I'm ready to offer absolution, but I don't think he'd appreciate the joke. Right now he needs more from me than levity, so I assure him that I feel much the same way. I tell him that I'm repeatedly drawn to the wild by an urge I don't fully understand. He nods his head. There's no need to go on. "Now we know there are at least two of us," I say. Then I dig a notebook out of my pack. I pull a loose sheet of paper from it and read: "We cannot be *normal* and *alive* at the same time." After pausing, I tell Limps that a French philosopher named E.M. Cioran wrote this once and it pretty much sums up how I see things.

"That's deep," he says with a smile creeping up his face.

"I suppose it is," I say, realizing that I ended up lightening the mood after all. "But so is the urge that compels us. We come out here looking for what our day-to-day lives can't provide."

"Maybe so," Limps responds. "All I know is that I have to come out here."

"Same here," I say. Then we drop the matter.

It's getting late. The long afternoon shadows that the trees have cast over the pond have grown longer. I sort through gear and consolidate my food into one bag. After that, I fire up my stove and boil water for dinner. Limps-a-Little lights his stove at the same time.

In the cool autumnal air, two thru-hikers enjoy dehydrated meals—one of the few luxuries of the trail. It's my last one before supplying at Long Lake. It's Limps first one ever. At seven bucks a pop, dehydrated meals seem a terrible extravagance to a man who does piecework for a living. But he picked up one just to see what it's like. Tastes pretty good, he tells me, and it sure makes dinner a simple affair. Pour a little hot water into the pouch, mix well, let it stand a few minutes, and voila! No dishes to clean afterward. Dinner doesn't get much easier than that.

Limps-a-Little strings his food bag in the trees a good distance away from the lean-to. I apologize for slinging mine so close to camp. Whatever. He doesn't care. We gather wood and soon have a roaring fire going. It's a lot bigger fire than I would make if I were alone, but what the heck. Companionship requires some accommodation. Limps heats with wood back home. He's been doing this as long as he can remember. So when he builds a fire, whether it's for heat, cooking, or just pleasure, he doesn't mess around.

"Have you seen any sign of porcupines?" Limps asks while looking around. No, I haven't. He read in his guidebook that porkies often visit this particular shelter. We should take care that our gear doesn't get chewed up. That reminds me of a shelter I stayed in once on Vermont's Long Trail. Every corner of it had been gnawed by those voracious critters. I slept that night with my hiking boots dangling over my head to protect them. Limps has an even better story.

It was the most miserable night he's ever spent on the trail. Limps landed in a Catskills lean-to late in the day, too tired to go any farther. "I saw those porcupine droppings and should've known better than to stay." But he did. Two porkies were living there. They chewed loudly on something half the night, making it impossible for him to sleep. And when finally they stopped chewing, they got beneath the lean-to floor and started making mad porky love. Limps cursed and growled as he repeatedly pounded on the floor, but that didn't stop them. Eventually, they finished their business and dozed off. But their heavy snoring kept him awake until dawn.

The sun leaves us. Darkness settles in. I bank the fire before calling it a night. Limps is already in his sleeping bag. He said he's not one to stay up late when he's on the trail. Fine by me. I settle into my sleeping bag, scribbling in my journal by lamplight, occasionally raising my pen long enough to exchange a few words with him. By eight o'clock, though, we agree to stop talking to each other. By eight-fifteen, Limps is sleeping. Soon I'm right behind him on that long, winding trail into the land of dreams.

TUESDAY, SEPTEMBER 12. Limps and I awaken about the same time. We are stiff, achy, and reluctant to get up. It was a frosty night last night and the relative warmth of the morning sun makes it hard to quit our sleeping bags. But eventually we take the plunge into chilly morning air. I've got fresh coffee brewing a few minutes later. It works its magic on us as the cool mist gradually burns away to a beautiful day. An hour later, we're both eager to get back on the trail.

Limps has a few coffee filters on hand—ones that he usually wraps around the intake of his water filter whenever he's tapping an especially dirty source. Knowing that my supply of coffee filters is short, he hands them to me. What the heck—his son will be picking him up at the Route 30 trailhead in a few hours, so he doesn't need them any more. I thank him, then carefully tuck the filters away.

We leave camp together. When the hundred-yard side trail tags the Northville-Placid Trail, Limps-a-Little turns south and I turn north. We exchange quick goodbyes as we separate. Then silence reigns. "That was a pleasant interlude," I say out loud, but now it's just me and the wild again. The trail hugging the pond is easy to follow. I listen to the click of my trekking poles as they bounce off roots and rocks, quickly losing myself in thought.

The lean-to at the northern end of Tirrell Pond is full of camping gear. Two large dome tents are pitched nearby. A campfire is smoldering but there's no one in sight. How odd. Looks like a half dozen people spent the night here. Where are they now? I didn't see anyone fishing from canoes while I was hiking around the pond. Whatever. I pass quietly through the camp, just in case someone's still sleeping in one of the zipped-up tents. Then I slip back into the woods.

The trail beyond the outfitter's camp is flat for the most part, so I make good time. I follow a set of deer tracks pressed deep into patches of mud. The forest around me is young. Probably logged not long ago. After skirting yet another wetland, the trail runs into a private, well-maintained, woods road. I follow it half a mile before the NPT markers veer sharply to the left, away from the road. From this junction the trail begins a long, steady ascent to a narrow pass. At three thousand feet, that pass is the highest point on the Northville-Placid Trail. The nine-hundred-foot climb just ahead is the biggest elevation change I'll face this trip. So I remove my pack and sit down on a large rock to rest a while before taking it on.

I'm in something of a funk right now. Not sure why. Part of it is a social hangover. Limps and I did a lot of talking. Part of it is probably due to sheer exhaustion. Day ten on the trail and I'm feeling it. Two cold nights without much sleep didn't help matters, either. A little rumbling in my gut to boot—a sure sign that something's not right down there. But there's more to this funk than the obvious. There's something else going on here, something simmering just below the surface of consciousness. I can feel a long, deep sadness building. It's a feeling that comes and goes with greater frequency as I grow older. I sit on the rock, sucking down water and trail mix, fighting off the same creeping sense of alienation that I was ready to laugh away yesterday afternoon when Limps-a-Little voiced it. But it's no laughing matter now.

Show me a solitary woods wanderer and I'll show you a bluesman. So much time alone gives one too much time to think, I suppose. "Why should pensiveness be akin to sadness?" Thoreau once asked himself in his journals. But in typical Thoreauvian contrariness, he was quick to add: "There is a certain fertile sadness which I would not avoid, but rather seek. It is positively joyful to me. It saves my life from being trivial." Ditto that. At the risk of sounding un-American, I believe there is more to life than the pursuit of happiness. Some of us require a deeper, more profound connection to the real, even if it ends up making us sad every once in a while. Whenever I prepare for a big outdoor adventure, I know there will come a moment like this on the trail when despair sweeps over me for no apparent reason. But I pack up my things and go, anyhow.

The recurrence of this backcountry funk over the years convinces me that there's something terribly real about the wild. While looking around from my rocky perch, absorbing the silence and stillness of the forest, I see something I don't often see. I see something I don't want to see. Call it a glimpse of eternity set against my own mortality. Call it harsh reality. Call it whatever you want. It's about the passage of time. The wild is eternal but life is fleeting, as everything in the forest attests. My life is no different in this regard. How can I make the most of my brief sojourn in this world? How can I make my life count? How can I live in a way that cuts deep, that goes beyond all the pat slogans and facile credos that stink up the lowlands?

At age fifty, while sitting on a rock, I sort what is of value from what is merely smoke. A loving spouse, family and friends, good work, good health, and being out here—these are the things that matter. Everything else is a bad joke. As I stare into oblivion, all the platitudes thrown at me by clergymen and ideologues over the years burst like soap bubbles. It's a glorious moment. I realize in a flash of insight that the wild is what keeps me anchored to the ineffable truth of the world. But I've had this insight before. Why do I have to keep coming out here like this? Why doesn't the lesson stick? Once again, that day-to-day routine of mine back in the lowlands has muddled my thoughts. Once again, I've been fooled into believing there's some substance behind the blather of advertisers and propagandists. And I hate myself for it. But why should I be any different from everyone else? We are all mesmerized by the brilliant glare of clever ideas, the glitz, the hype. A trip out here sets things right, though. This green infinity is no bullshit. Yeah, *this* is what's real. With that thought, I hoist the heavy pack to my shoulders and move on.

My slow, steady pace makes the climb a relatively easy one. I stop frequently to drink water and catch my breath. I spook several grouse during the ascent. Or perhaps I should say, they spook me. While passing through a large clearing, I look for the bear prints that Limps-a-Little said he saw here. I find one, I think, but am not sure about it. I stop and look around in the middle of the clearing, hoping to catch a flash of black fur. No bear shows itself, though. Of course not. Wild animals rarely appear on cue.

Beyond the clearing, the trail becomes steeper. Sweating even more now, I'm grateful for the bubbling spring that suddenly appears on my left—the one mentioned in my guidebook. A blink of the eye and I would've missed it. I stop to fill both of my bottles with cold, clear water. I gulp down as much as I can, then resume the climb.

The higher I go, the more I advance into autumn. The canopy overhead has turned deep shades of gold, orange, and red. During the last few hundred feet of the ascent, conifers take over. The notch at the top of the long ridge, nestled between two nameless summits, is positively boreal—nothing but spruces and firs. I pass through the notch as if passing from one world into another. Then I follow the ridge eastward a short while. It's still gradually ascending. On the height of land, I cry out "Oh God!" at the sight of two hikers sitting in the middle of the trail, eating lunch. I laugh nervously, hoping they didn't hear the remark. Then I say "Hi" in as pleasant a tone as I can muster. Naturally, we strike up a conversation.

Chapter 14

MID-AFTERNOON. I drop my pack in the middle of the trail, ten feet away from the couple, then reach for my water bottle. I exchange a few banalities with them before pulling out my food bag. Backwoods encounters like this are always tenuous. But Bruce and Marty are so relaxed and open that asking to join them for lunch seems a mere formality. Soon all three of us are sitting on the trail, munching away, laughing and talking as if we're old friends. It's an unexpected turn of events.

Bruce and Marty are headed south, on their way back to their car after hiking north over this ridge to Long Lake. They are seasoned backpackers about my age who, like me, are hiking the Northville-Placid Trail end-to-end. But unlike me, they're doing it piecemeal. This time they're out for three days. Next time, who knows? They have no strict itinerary. In a half dozen outings, they've already hiked from Benson to Long Lake. Eventually they'll do the entire NPT, but there's no rush. Bruce is a retired schoolteacher. Marty is a traveling nurse who can get work anywhere, anytime, so they're free to do whatever they want. Earlier this year, they were in Montana. Before that, somewhere in the Deep South. They have that ideal combination of freedom and economic security that most people only dream about. I'm impressed by it, anyhow.

After regaling me with tales of hiking adventures in different places around the country, they listen attentively to my stories. I talk up Vermont's Long Trail, of course, but they're more interested in Pharaoh Lake, John's Brook, and other Adirondack destinations. They're especially interested in the off-the-beaten-track places that I mention. Bruce and Marty don't like crowds. That's why autumn is their favorite season to hike. Thousands of people take to the trails during the summer, but hardly anyone comes out this time of year—at least not in the middle of the week. Yeah, Bruce and Marty have complete freedom, and they're making the most of it.

They are surprised by my wealth of knowledge about the area. How have I found the time to visit so many different places? I tell them that I used to work as a hiking guide for a tour company. In fact, I was a bona fide Adirondack guide for a few years, registered with the DEC and all that. Even had a badge to prove it. Bruce and Marty are duly impressed. They're a bit too impressed, I think, so I explain that it's not that hard to become a registered Adirondack guide. It's just a matter of paying a fee and taking a test that any second-class Boy Scout could pass. A couple first aid certifications, a water safety course, a physical, and you're there. Being an Adirondack guide today isn't like being one in the old days. No, not like that at all.

IT'S HARD TO IMAGINE a college professor like Ebenezer Emmons or a newspaperman like Charles Fenno Hoffman venturing deep into the Adirondacks in the 1830s without a seasoned woodsman like John Cheney leading the way. Ralph Waldo Emerson and his effete, intellectual companions wouldn't have considered going into the wild without assistance. That renowned Adirondack writer, William H.H. Murray, couldn't say enough good things about his guide. Neither could another writer, Charles Dudley Warner, who practically canonized his backcountry companion, Orson

"Old Mountain" Phelps. According to Warner, Phelps was "a true citizen of the wilderness." Such a man, Warner claimed, is not so much a lover of nature as a part of it.

John Cheney, Orson Phelps, John Plumley, Alvah Dunning, Mitchell Sabattis—these were some of the Adirondack guides whose reputations have reached mythical proportions over the years. These were the woodsmen whose company meant as much to the people they guided as the wild country itself. A few nineteenth century guides, like Sabattis, were Native Americans, but most were just working-class stiffs who had learned how to scratch a living from the Adirondacks one way or another. All of them were lauded for their hunting and fishing skills, camp craft, endurance, and near-mystical knowledge of the woods. They were the gods of the forest. All of them were *independent* guides, of course. Hotel guides were another matter. By comparison, hotel guides were lazy, incompetent opportunists who preyed on unsuspecting tourists. No doubt their shortcomings have been exaggerated over time, but mythology is like that. After all, the feats of gods must tower over those of mere mortals in order to merit our highest esteem.

Perceptions changed during the twentieth century. Would Bob and George Marshall have been able to hike the High Peaks without Herbert Clark showing them the way? Not likely, yet we remember the Marshall brothers in all their vigor to protect the wild, not the older, simpler hireling who introduced them to it. The same can be said of modern-day pathfinders. The Adirondack guide has gradually diminished in stature, as the wilderness has become less threatening and more accessible.

Thanks to automobiles and interstate highways, nature-lovers invaded the Adirondacks en masse during the 1960s. Tens of thousands of college kids and other outdoor enthusiasts took to the trails on their own accord, with little or no assistance. They relied upon trail blazes, topographical maps, guidebooks, and state-of-the-art backpacking gear. As a consequence, the guide became a specialist of sorts: a whitewater guide, a rock-climbing guide, a naturalist, a hunting and fishing guide, and so forth. Nowadays, Adirondack guides are still valued as teachers but are no longer considered backwoods gurus. No, those days are gone.

While guiding small groups during the 1990s, I had to have many of the same tools as my predecessors: first aid training, survival skills, the ability to navigate by map and compass, and a working knowledge of the woods. But the clientele had changed considerably. Or had it? Most of my clients were middle-aged urbanites who had never been in the forest before and had no real understanding of it. Some things never change, I suppose. Although modern-day guides are more teachers than anything else, they still perform the same basic function as those old timers. During my short tenure as a guide, I introduced hundreds of newcomers to the wild. And that's a time-honored tradition.

AFTER SAYING GOODBYE to Bruce and Marty, I follow the ridge a while longer, hoping for a break in the trees and a good view northward. No such luck. The trail turns sharply, then drops down the north slope of the ridge. The ground is steep here, very steep. Glad I didn't have to come up this way. But going down is easy enough. Soon I'm out of the dark conifers and back in the broadleaf trees. A half hour into the descent, the trail levels out a bit and a brook appears on my left. Now hiking is a breeze. The gold, yellow, and orange leaves in the trees around me are a joy to behold. And the steady roar of water crashing over rocks lifts my spirits.

I follow the brook another half hour before reaching a wooden bridge. I noted this stream crossing last night while studying my maps. This is where I had planned on camping tonight and, sure enough, there's a beautiful, flat campsite right next the bridge. Unfortunately, there's a "No

Camping" sign posted over it. The DEC has been here. Hmm…the sign looks rather absurd, plastered as it is to a tree in the middle of nowhere. I can't help but laugh. I'm tempted to ignore the sign and camp here anyway, but decide against it. Clearly this campsite has been used too much. Besides, it's too close to the brook. So I hike down the trail another fifty yards, away from the brook, dropping my heavy load on the next available piece of flat real estate. This'll do.

My camp this evening is a modest affair: a pitched tarp, a backpack strapped to the trunk of a small birch, and a food bag slung from the branch of a large maple not far away. I walk back to the brook to fetch water. In a couple hours, I'll fire up my stove and cook up some ramen noodles. Ramen is an old standby, quick and easy. Since I'm camped so close to the trail, I won't mess around with a fire. That way no one will ever know that I've been here. Although I come to the woods to do whatever I please, I'm a firm believer in having as little visible impact upon the land as possible.

The sun drops behind the shoulder of Mt. Sabattis well before dusk. In the couple remaining hours of shady daylight, I lounge on my foam pad. It was designed for sleeping, but it makes a good seat when propped against a tree. I write a short letter to Judy—one that I'll mail at Long Lake tomorrow—then scribble in my journal. I take stock of my physical condition, noting all my sores, cuts, rashes, and general aches. Trivial stuff, really. All things considered, I'm in remarkably good shape at the end of my tenth day on the trail. There's no reason why I can't keep moving north after picking up supplies in Long Lake. Eighty-five miles of trail pounding and I'm no worse for wear. Even a fifty-year-old body can be resilient, I guess.

Before calling it a night, I look up through an opening in the forest canopy. There's nothing but blue sky directly overhead, so I probably don't need to pitch my tarp any lower to the ground. The tarp won't provide much protection from the elements the way it's set up right now, but I don't think it'll rain tonight. I don't bother covering my backpack, either. "You worry too much," I scold myself while brushing my teeth. Then I go to bed early.

THREE A.M. I awaken to the sound of raindrops hitting the tarp. Only the faintest precipitation is coming down right now, but that could change. Dammit! Why didn't I secure my camp better? I burrow deep into my sleeping bag, hoping the drizzle will stop, but the splattering sound above my head steadily increases. I get up and scramble about camp in darkness and dampness, cursing myself while fixing the mistake.

By the time I've covered my backpack and lowered the tarp, the rain is coming down hard. Now I'm soaked. I dry off the best I can while crawling back under the tarp. I pull my things away from the tarp's edges to keep them from getting wet. I draw up the bottom of my sleeping bag, as well. This forces me into a fetal position with most of my belongings tucked between my thighs and chest. The tarp is too short—that's all there is to it. Months ago I knew the tarp had been cut short when I first took it out of its packaging. Did I return it? Hell no. Instead I told myself that I'd just have to be careful about how I set it up. Well, that was a real brain cramp, and Mother Nature isn't forgiving it. So here I am, all scrunched up and waiting for daylight, too uncomfortable to sleep.

Chapter 15

DAYBREAK. I'm up and breaking camp in dismal, grey light. A steady rain is falling so I stash all my things beneath the tarp and carefully wipe down each piece of gear before stuffing it into my pack. By the time I hoist the heavy, wet load to my shoulders, the forest is as bright as it's going to be this morning. A thick mist envelops the trees. An unrelenting rain pelts their leaves. I grab my trekking poles and commence the two-mile hike to State Route 28.

Breakfast is an energy bar eaten on the run. No coffee. I'll get that later on this morning in the village of Long Lake. I don't like trying to function without coffee, much less trying to hike, but firing up the camp stove would have been too much trouble. Besides, the prospect of standing around drinking coffee in the rain didn't appeal to me. So here I am uncaffeinated and making tracks. It's not so bad, really. I'm hiking fast and strong. The cheap, vinyl poncho I'm wearing is keeping me cool and somewhat dry. No, not so bad at all.

Fresh deer tracks underfoot convince me that I'm not alone, even though there isn't a creature in sight—neither deer, nor bird, nor chipmunk. It's kind of lonely out here, actually. But I'm hiking fast so it hardly matters. In fact, I'm hiking too fast. I'm not so much *in* the forest right now as I am *passing through* it. On the other hand, I don't feel like dallying. It's raining, I'm already a little damp, and there are a host of creature comforts to be had in Long Lake.

Just about the time I enter a large spruce grove, I start hearing the rumble of trucks in the distance. The trail underfoot is soft and muddy between short stretches of puncheon. Suddenly I'm on a long, unbroken run of new boardwalk cutting through the conifers. The forest floor around me is a sea of Kelly green moss brought to life by the rain—a cheery sight on this otherwise dismal day. The sound of truck traffic grows louder and louder until finally I'm standing next to a road. A quick water break, along with another energy bar, then down the road I go—headed west.

Walking the gravel shoulder of the paved road is no fun at all. The passing trucks and cars are incredibly loud and obnoxious. Most of them spray me with a cold, dirty mist as they roar past. I've switched from the cheap poncho to my regular raingear but it makes little difference. The combined forces of wind, rain, and my own sweat make the roadside walk a wet one. I'm moving incredibly fast now and it's only a mile and a half walk into town, so I should be there soon. But thirty minutes under conditions like these seems a lot longer. When finally I reach the convenience store in the middle of town, I drop my pack and slip indoors without a moment's hesitation. The sudden blast of dry heat stuns me.

Inside the store, I pick up lip balm, zip-lock bags, and a few necessities. The clerk behind the counter is kind enough to give me half a dozen coffee filters free of charge so I don't have to buy an "economy" package of 150. I land at one of the plastic tables and suck down a bottle of apple juice between sips of piping hot coffee. The people drifting in and out of the store are in a frame of mind completely different from mine. They're all going about their business, locked in familiar patterns, oblivious to the harsh elements. I'm all wet and still in the woods. There's a guy on a small television screen eight feet away telling anyone who will listen just how great this store is. It's all rather bizarre. I try to ignore my surroundings, gazing out the window at Mother Nature instead. She is patiently waiting for me to come back out and play. Then it occurs to me that I like being in this warm, dry store so much that I'd better get out of here fast. If I stay much longer, my trek will end right now. I grab my coffee and finish it outside.

The big general store across the street is called Hoss's Country Corner. I find a section full of practical things like camp candles, bug spray, and rubberized raingear. I pick up a 6-by-8 tarp to replace my 5-by-7 one. Soon I'm forking over a few bucks and some change for it. Amazing. Hard to believe that something so useful could be so inexpensive. My rough night last night was entirely uncalled for.

I leave Hoss's, hiking farther west up the road until I reach the post office. There I make my third and last stop before retracting my steps back to the NPT. A cheery postal clerk hands me the parcel that I mailed "general delivery" to myself nearly a month ago. I take the box over to the empty corner of the lobby where I dropped my pack and open it as if opening a treasure chest. What a beautiful sight to behold: a four-day supply of food, some clean clothing, a small container of medicated powder, and other amenities. I transfer it all to my pack then stuff a bag full of trash, some hopelessly dirty clothes, and my mosquito bar into the box before sealing it up. This late in the season, I figure the mosquito bar isn't necessary. That's what I'm gambling on, anyhow.

After mailing the box back home, along with a letter to Judy, I exit the post office. A sheet of rain greets me as I step outside. That's okay. While the walk out of town is just as miserable as the one into it was, at least now I'm caffeinated and fully supplied. In fact, I'm in pretty good spirits. It's nice knowing that everything I need to finish my trek is now on my back. The High Peaks Wilderness, only a couple miles up the road, is all that stands between me and Lake Placid. I'm quite pleased by the prospect. As much as I preach the importance of being *in* the forest instead of *passing through* it, I enjoy completing a task as much as anyone does. And backpacking a hundred-plus miles of rough trail is no mean feat for a guy my age.

THE TRAILHEAD FOR THE HIGH PEAKS WILDERNESS AREA is located just off Tarbell Hill Road, half a mile uphill from Route 28. I drop my pack right after signing into the trail register, then rest a bit before continuing north. It's still raining. I drink half a liter of water and consume yet another energy bar while wiping sweat from my face with an already soaked bandana. Hard to tell now what is sweat and what is rain. I'm wet, that's all I know for sure, and the air temperature is somewhere around sixty degrees. I'd better not linger here. Don't want to get chilled.

While looking around, I notice a rather large sign posted right below the trailhead register. It's a wonder that I didn't notice it while signing in. The DEC is promoting the use of bear resistant canisters—those cylindrical, hard plastic food containers designed to confound pesky animals. Beneath a photo of a bear halfway up a tree and reaching for a food bag, the DEC announces to the world that it has proposed a regulation making such canisters mandatory in the eastern part of the High Peaks. This proposal was accepted in 2005. I guess that means it's a law now. This is the first official word I've received about the matter, though my ADK guidebook mentioned that bear canisters are required in some places. My guidebook also informed me that NPT thru-hikers are exempt from this rule. It's all very confusing.

Bear canisters are a good idea. I won't argue with that. The bears around here have been raiding backpackers' food supplies for years, and these canisters successfully foil their efforts. But they're heavy and bulky. Since bulk and weight are the two biggest challenges every long-distance hiker faces when packing for a trip, most don't mess around with bear cans. Besides, eighty bucks is a lot of money to shell out for what is essentially a large plastic jar. More to the point, though, it's not necessary. I suspect that for every food bag plucked from the trees by a particularly resourceful bear, twenty are taken on the ground with little effort. For the past thirty-five years, I've slung my food in the trees without incident. And now the DEC is telling me I have to use a canister because too many lazy, unwary backpackers have been feeding the bears. It rubs me the wrong way.

In his highly informative book, *Bear Attacks: Their Causes and Avoidance*, Stephen Herrero noted that ninety percent of all injuries to people by black bears during a twenty-year period were due to habituation. The research I did on the Internet this summer backs up this claim. Habituation is just a fancy word for wild animals getting used to being around people and gleaning food from them. When bears develop this habit, they become a problem—a *big* problem. The campground at Marcy Dam, which is a big jump-off point for hikers exploring the High Peaks, is famous for bear trouble of this sort. I've been hearing about it for decades. With this in mind, I cut the DEC some slack. It's good to know that someone is finally addressing the issue. I just wish their solution didn't have to make my life more difficult.

ONE LAST MILE OF RAIN-SOAKED TRAIL, then I'm done for the day. I arrive at the Catlin Bay lean-to early in the afternoon, happy to find it empty. After dropping my bag, I tour the sprawling, high-impact tenting area around the shelter, looking for other campers. Nobody. This is obviously a hot spot in the summer for both backpackers hiking the trail and canoeists coming off Long Lake, but right now it's a ghost town. I've got the whole place to myself. The lake lives up to its name, stretching as far as I can see. Long Lake village is only a couple miles south of here, but you'd never know it. There are a few cabins on the far side of the lake. Otherwise the shoreline is wild and undeveloped. Most of this side of the lake is designated wilderness.

It takes about an hour to string lines inside the lean-to and hang all my wet gear. If any hikers come along and join me, it'll be a job making room for them. Okay, maybe it would only be a minor inconvenience. In fact, I wouldn't mind the company. It's a grey day and nothing is quite as lonely as an empty camping area. Whatever. Right now, I'm just glad to be out of the rain and drying out my things. I'm even happier once I get into some dry clothes.

While sorting through my newly acquired supplies, I sniff the clean t-shirt that I retrieved from the Long Lake parcel. Its soapy smell is absolutely heavenly. So is the taste of the beef jerky that I packed along with it. The jerky is the centerpiece of my midday meal. Funny how something I wouldn't normally eat at home tastes so good out here. This is what a hardworking body wants, I suppose—salt and protein. Not that I'm an expert when it comes to nutrition. The jerked meat is a pleasant change from an otherwise bland diet, that's all I know.

Once lunch is over and the food bag is slung, there isn't much else to do. That's my excuse, anyhow, for unrolling my sleeping bag and crawling into it. The rain is still coming down, and I can't resist the prospect of being both dry *and* warm. I scribble in my journal for a while but doze off in the middle of a sentence. Hiked only seven miles today but am tired from last night's fiasco. Now's the time to make up for lost sleep.

Chapter 16

THE LOUD, HOARSE CROAK of a raven stirs me from my afternoon slumber. Along with the mist and cool rain, the sound reminds me of Southeast Alaska. But the dark, woody lean-to in which I'm nestled is very northeastern, as is the surrounding forest. That is, it *looks* northeastern to me. There's no mistaking the smell of it, anyhow. I get up and check the clothes strung across the lean-to interior to see if they've dried out. Not really. But the rain has diminished to thin drizzle so I'm hoping the sky will clear soon. That would help.

"What the hell…" The sudden appearance of two hikers startles me. They're walking a path less than twenty yards away from camp. It's a man and woman about my age. "Hi," they say. I return the greeting. They stop and ask the usual questions: Where are you coming from? Where are you going? How long are you out here? I answer their questions but am not very friendly about it. After they announce that they're camped near the other lean-to, a quarter mile south, they invite me to join them for dinner. I decline, saying that I'm nice and dry in this shelter right now and think I'll just stay this way. They understand, of course, but their faces still register disappointment. There aren't many opportunities out here to socialize. We exchange goodbyes, then they continue down the trail. I regret my decision as soon as they disappear.

Down by the lakeshore, I collect enough water for the evening. Ravens call out repeatedly while I'm doing so. A few waterfowl fly past, too far away to identify. The rain has stopped, but grey clouds still cover the sky. A large, reddish-brown newt crawls through the rocks a few feet away. The wild is all around me. The wild is within me. By the time I've filled both my water bottles, it occurs to me that I'm much more comfortable being out here than I was back in the village. Yet I'm longing for company.

Dinner is a remarkably easy affair, thanks to an efficient little camp stove and the luxury of yet another dehydrated meal. I eat it directly from the package so there's no cleanup. By the time I've finished, my body heat has dried out the pants I'm wearing. I have a thermal shirt on beneath my rain jacket so I'm quite comfortable right now. Why not go a-visiting? I sling my food bag, grab the headlamp, then head for my neighbor's place.

BOB AND LYNN HAVE ESTABLISHED a rather elaborate camp atop a wooded knoll on a spit of land jutting into the lake. Because they came here by canoe, they have a lot more gear than any backpacker would ever dream of carrying. I approach their camp cautiously, making sure that I'm still welcome. They greet me with broad smiles and warm "hellos," glad to have company. I settle onto a makeshift stool in the center of camp where Lynn is situated. Bob asks if I'd like a cup of coffee. When I say "yes," he immediately sets to work. Lynn offers me a homemade brownie. I feel like royalty.

Bob and Lynn are retired. They have been hiking and canoeing in the Adirondacks since Labor Day. I ask if they've run into a couple of hikers named Bruce and Marty, and yes, in fact, they have. Very nice folks. I mention Limps-a-Little, describe him in detail and, yes, they think they ran into him a couple days ago as well. What a small world it is out here this time of year. Yes, a small world indeed. So small that it's beginning to feel like an exclusive club.

Bob putters around camp while Lynn does most of the talking. She tells me that they're from Pennsylvania. They often visit the Adirondacks. In fact, they've climbed all but nine of its forty-six highest peaks. Yeah, they took it that far before calling it quits. The peak trails are too busy. Bob and Lynn prefer places a little less traveled. Have they been to West Canada Lakes Wilderness? They certainly have. "That's wild country," Lynn says, then she recounts how they took a side trail once and ended up in a remote place called Lost Pond.

"Lost Pond!" I blurt out. I can't believe she just said that. But when I carefully describe it, Lynn convinces me that they've been to the same place I have. "You're the only people I've ever met who have been there," I say in amazement. Then I tell them how I bushwhacked north from Lost Pond back in '02 with my dog in tow, as the trail shown on my old map disappeared into the brush. They both laugh. They got turned around there, too. They must've had the same map. And after looking an hour or so for that missing trail, they ended up going back the way they came.

"Have any idea what the weather's going to be like the next couple of days?" I ask. In response to this, Bob pulls out a radio and turns it on. The static coming from it disrupts the forest quiet, but all three of us are curious about what lies ahead. Eventually Bob finds a station giving a weather report. Looks like there's more rain in the forecast for tomorrow. Things should dry out by the weekend, though. What day is this? Wednesday. Oh yeah, Wednesday, of course. Rain tomorrow, ending Friday. I can live with that. So can they.

Darkness descends. Bob fires up a lantern. We talk a little more about the Adirondacks, each of us telling more stories. Then we dance around some sensitive political issues and flirt with religion for a while before getting back to common ground. So it goes out here. Just by virtue of being in the woods, we have this much in common. The wild itself is the great leveler, valued by everyone who comes out here. Everything else is dicey.

I'd like to stay and talk more, but it's getting dark. The journey back to camp is going to be hard enough as it is, so I get up to leave. I say good-bye to my newfound friends, thanking them for their hospitality, then slip away. I grope through the night, back towards my lean-to by the pale beam of my headlamp. I get turned around more than once in the thick mist, but eventually find my way home.

I fire up a candle as soon as I reach the shelter, more for solace than light. It illuminates the lean-to's interior—an inviting sight—as I go about my bedtime routine. But there's still something rather disarming about the dark, dripping forest all around me. While brushing my teeth over the campfire pit, I can just barely see Bob and Lynn's lantern light in the distance, all by itself in the darkness like a ship's beacon at sea. I miss them already. Guess I'm more in the mood to socialize than I thought. That's good because I'm likely to encounter more people tomorrow. The High Peaks are always busy. Then again, this time of year, who knows?

A SOLITARY LOON AWAKENS ME in the middle of the night but falls silent just as quickly. Then two barred owls start hooting incessantly, keeping me from getting back to sleep. They hoot back and forth through the eerie quiet, carrying on a protracted conversation about god-knows-what while I lie on the shelter floor listening helplessly. I wonder what it's like to be an owl and live mostly in darkness. At night they see what I can only imagine. Same goes for what the bear smells and the deer hears. Despite my attraction to wild nature, I am still more a creature of my abstractions—more gray matter between the ears than anything else. Yeah, when it comes to brains, my species hit the jackpot. So why are owls considered wise? Perhaps not all wisdom is cerebral.

Chapter 17

THURSDAY MORNING, SEPTEMBER FOURTEENTH. A light drizzle commences as I'm leaving Catlin Bay lean-to. Half a mile down the trail, it builds to a steady shower. I'm not happy about this. I've seen enough water for one trip, thank you very much. Fortunately, my gear is mostly dry now so I'm in better shape than I was this time yesterday. Let it rain then. It won't stop me. This section of the NPT, cutting through the High Peaks Wilderness, is thirty-five miles long, and I'm determined to knock off a third of it today. I'm supplied, rested, and ready to go.

"Every walk is a sort of crusade," Thoreau wrote in an essay once. That pretty much sums up my frame of mind right now. I plant my trekking poles with unshakeable resolve, scoffing under my breath at the rain. Here we go again: endless green forest, mud holes, and incessant dampness. But this time the terrain is working to my advantage. That's no small consolation. I'm moving fast down a relatively flat, easy trail. For the next six miles, it follows the shoreline—sometimes a couple hundred yards away from the lake, sometimes right along the water's edge. I should be able to reach Cold River without too much difficulty. I'll reach it before sundown, certainly.

What do I have to prove? Absolutely nothing. I'm on a crusade, yes, but one that wouldn't make any sense to most people. I'm crusading for the wild itself. I'm going all the way, going as deep as I can go for as long as possible. I've done this before and am doing it again. It's a mad passion, certainly, to sweat and grunt deeper into the forest, hoping for some scrap of earthy enlightenment, however fleeting. It's a crusade, certainly, but one that's just a little desperate. I know what the wild has to offer, but also know that the most ecstatic moments one can experience out here can't be forced. All I can do is go deeper, losing myself in the simple joys and miseries of the trail, hoping that some unforeseen turn of events will make it all worthwhile.

Thoreau walked to save himself from the crass commercialism of his day. He cherished the smallest nuggets of natural insight that arose during his walks. I, on the other hand, am considerably more ambitious. I long for an insight into the universe at large, for a glimpse of God. Tall order, no doubt, but I experience something close to it every once in a great while. Sometimes I am *profoundly* surprised. If I'm resolute and receptive, that is. If not, well, then at least I'll get some exercise. Like Thoreau, I can only take whatever the wild throws my way. After all, I have no control over it. The wild is, by definition, beyond my control. I can only wait patiently for something to happen, poised in a state of readiness like a fisherman with a line in the water, waiting for a strike.

BY THE TIME I REACH KELLY POINT, the rain has subsided. I stop at one of two lean-tos for a short break and a long stretch of the muscles before continuing north. I chug down a half liter of water, alarmed by my own thirst, alarmed by how much I'm sweating despite the cool rain. I'm hiking hard—maybe too hard. With that in mind, I cut my pace a bit while departing Kelly Point. Can't keep up a three-mile-an-hour pace all day. Besides, there's really no reason to rush. I have nothing else to do today other than hike, and twelve miles isn't that far to go.

Just beyond Kelly Point, I run across a southbound hiker named Kim.

He stops in the middle of the trail to converse. He's a lean, middle-aged fellow with a pack as big as mine. Two young women and a small dog accompany him. One of the young women calls him Dad, so that much about them is clear. When I tell Kim that I'm thru-hiking, he asks how my trek has gone so far. He's surprised when I say "good," so I moderate my answer with a few complaints about mud holes and rotten puncheon. Kim says this is his fourth time hiking the NPT end-to-end. I find that hard to believe, even though he looks *physically* capable of doing so. And his companions? The girls are going only as far as Long Lake. After that he'll be on his own.

"Are you carrying a bear can?" I ask out of curiosity.

"Sure am," he says while beaming a smile. "It's great! No more tossing ropes up trees and getting all tangled up. I don't miss dealing with that. The can keeps chipmunks and mice out of my food, too. They can climb trees as well as bears, you know. Besides, it's portable furniture. It makes a good seat when I'm in camp. "

"Huh. That's interesting," I respond. Then, with a heavy sigh, I tell Kim that I'll probably be packing one on my next trip into these woods. He says I'll be glad I did.

ANOTHER MILE DOWN THE TRAIL, I come to a break in the forest. Here a small stream trickles out of a new beaver pond. I look around for wildlife but see only vegetation. Not a creature in sight. All the same, I fantasize about encountering a moose or a bear while continuing my hike. Then my foot slips off a short stretch of moss-covered puncheon and the next thing I know, I'm heading for the ground. It's a soft landing in mud, thank heaven, but the fall only adds to my general state of grunginess. Now one whole side of me is wet and dirty.

A short while later, I encounter something that's pretty rare in deep woods, especially on a day like this. Three inexperienced-looking women carrying full backpacks suddenly appear in front of me. I can hardly believe my eyes. They're stumbling around in the mud but aren't falling down as I did. They look ready for a break, so I stop and chat with them even though I just socialized with Kim. They pull out bottles of tea as they chatter away, animated, seemingly oblivious to the gloomy forest all around them. I can't help but wonder if there's something else in their bottles. They seem unduly happy for a day like this one.

One of the jolly ladies proudly announces that she's in her sixties. Then she tells me that her friend is in her fifties and her daughter is in her forties. They aren't athletic or particularly woodsy. I wonder why they're out here. After asking a few questions, I learn that they're part of a larger group on an annual outing. The three of them hiked up from Long Lake yesterday and spent the night at Plumley's camp, a mile and a half north of here. Now they're on their way back down to Kelly Point where they'll join the rest of the group tonight. Everyone else is coming by boat, but these intrepid ladies wanted a little adventure. So here they are. They seem to be having the time of their lives.

I notice that one of them has patched a rip in her cheap vinyl poncho with duct tape. I tell her that I patched my poncho the same way, adding with feigned snobbishness: "Duct tape is *haute couture* on the trail." All three ladies howl with delight. Yessir, I've struck a chord. Trail levity is something I cultivated years ago while working as a hiking guide. Suddenly it occurs to me that some of the people I have guided into the woods in years past must be going out on their own as these women are. I feel good about this. The wilderness isn't just for hardcore hikers like me. It belongs to everyone. These ladies are proof of that. I wish them a pleasant hike to Kelly Point, then continue on my way north. The sound of laughter slowly fades into the forest behind me.

PLUMLEY'S IS THE NORTHERNMOST camping area on Long Lake. I'm sure that it's used a great deal by boaters. While not as big and sprawling as Catlin Bay, there must be plenty of activity here during the summer. This outpost consists of two lean-tos and half a dozen well-worn campsites. The beach has been etched by the bows of canoes and other small boats. There's a makeshift landing here, too—a small, rocky wharf protruding a few yards into the lake. Primitive yet no less effective. I drop my pack then pull out my food bag. A motorboat roars past as I settle along the shoreline to eat lunch.

I read somewhere that Long Lake is the birthplace of the Adirondack guideboat. In my mind's eye I can see John Plumley landing here over a hundred years ago, with some wealthy hunter or fisherman from the city. No doubt he told many tales while sitting around a campfire here. No doubt he gave hundreds of urbanites their first real taste of the wild. That was back in the day, of course. The world has changed considerably since then, but these woods and waters remain largely the same. And right now, as I gaze across placid, grey waters rippling beneath an overcast sky, that continuity seems like a great blessing.

NORTH OF PLUMLEY'S, the trail climbs slowly out of a wet spot and up a large, unnamed hill covered with broadleaf trees—birch, beech, and maple. A thick mist shrouds the still forest, stirring my imagination. Any minute now, I expect to see a bear, coyote, or deer darting out of the dripping undergrowth, showing that mild sense of apprehension common to all wild animals. I search the mud beneath my feet for tracks. Surprisingly enough, I find nothing there. Even boot prints are rare on this particular stretch of trail.

The sound of my own heavy breathing underscores a creeping sense of isolation. Not loneliness but alone-ness, as if the woody realm I've just entered couldn't possibly accommodate more than one human being at a time. It's a feeling I've known only a few other times in my life, and only in the deepest woods. It's a feeling I find both attractive and repulsive—what is most unpleasant about being alone in the wild, yet precisely what draws me out here time and time again.

While gradually descending the far side of the hill, the landscape changes significantly. Now the trees are mostly conifers, with only a smattering of birches and maples among them. Now it's the kind of terrain where one wouldn't expect to see an animal: wide-open forest floor with little vegetation, heavily pocketed by wet spots. Large white pines dominate, which seems appropriate since the stream I'm fast approaching is called Pine Brook. The mist has cleared out but it's raining again. Ignoring the rain, I take a short break. My pack feels particularly heavy this afternoon, and the kick I got from the energy bars consumed at Plumley's is long gone. I think I'm wearing out in a big way. No matter. I'll only be on the trail a few days more.

A short while later, I spot a blue NPT disc nailed to a tree directly ahead, in the middle of a brand new beaver pond. A set of ribbons marks a temporary trail going around the pond. It's a five-minute detour at most. No big deal. Still, it makes me wonder what the trail ahead is going to be like. According to my map, it cuts across flat, boggy ground. Beaver country. Could be challenging, and, quite frankly, I'm not up for it. Right now I want effortless walking. I've traveled over nine miles today, I'm tired, and I just want to glide into camp. But the last few miles of any long hiking day are always the hardest.

My boots remain dry as I rock-hop across Pine Brook. A few wet, muddy spots in the trail beyond the stream soak them anyway. Oh well. My feet are in good shape for the most part, so I don't really care. I use my trekking poles to vault over and around the worst spots, taking the muddy slips and slides in stride. It's a wet year, and the inclement weather lately has really brought that point home.

Another beaver pond obstructs my passage. The detour around it looks like a permanent one. It's short enough, though. On the other side of the pond, I spot a large, new beaver lodge. Then I see something brown moving through the water. It's a beaver working in the middle of the day, curiously enough, seemingly indifferent to my intrusion. I stop and watch it for a while. I drop my pack and go down to the water's edge for a better look. I take a picture with my cheap, disposable camera as the creature swims about. It's a precious moment—one of those extended encounters with wildlife that borders upon the mystical. Am I making too much of it? Perhaps. But right now it seems like the wild itself is speaking to me. And the orange patches of maple leaves among dense conifers on the other side of the pond seem remarkably bright beneath the formless, light grey sky.

This has been a beaver kind of day. There are beaver ponds all over these woods. I can't hike a mile without coming upon the handiwork of those industrious creatures. It's hard to believe that this large, flat-tailed rodent was trapped close to extinction during the nineteenth century. They certainly have made a comeback. Now they are everywhere, and just as busy as ever. Where are their natural enemies? Why don't the coyotes hunt them down? No doubt their moated, woody fortresses keep them safe from whatever trouble is afoot. Beavers are quite clever when you think about it. Who else sculpts the land in such a dramatic way? Only humans. I'm impressed by the beaver's ability to radically alter its environment. I wonder how much these creatures think and plan as we do. Not quite the same, certainly. Still I wonder. My feet have been soaked countless times because of them.

SHATTUCK CLEARING WAS A BUSY LOGGING CAMP on the banks of Cold

River a century ago. Now it's a grassy slope. Here I reach the hundred-mile mark of my trek. This calls for a celebration. I drop my two-ton pack on the ground, noting my accomplishment with a deep breath exhaled, a swig of water, and yet another energy bar. Then I move on.

The trail becomes an easy-to-travel woods road as it slowly descends to the river. When finally I set foot upon the suspension bridge crossing Cold River, a smile breaks across my face. Made it! Now all I have to do is locate lean-to #3. On the other side of the river, I spot lean-to #4 right away. Turning south along the river and walking past it, I look for the other one. I go a couple hundred yards down a side trail and there it is. And it's all mine for the night. I drop my pack for the last time today and immediately sling a line for my food bag in a nearby tree. Thus ends an eleven-and-a-half-mile slog. Whew! That was harder than I thought it would be.

Chapter 18

COLD RIVER LEAN-TO #3 is ideally placed. It's perched atop a steep bank overlooking a sharp bend in the river. I can see the suspension bridge several hundred yards upstream from here. The shelter has a nice stone fireplace in front of it and a picnic table nearby. It's exceptionally tidy, as well. Almost too tidy. Firewood is scarce here and the ground beneath the surrounding conifers has been picked clean. No matter. I'm too tired to mess around with a campfire anyhow. Think I'll just go down to the river and clean up a bit. A short, steep trail leads to a little stone beach. It looks inviting.

While pumping water and washing up, it dawns on me that Cold River isn't just another backwoods stream. This is a bona fide river, about twenty to thirty yards wide and several feet deep in places. A tremendous amount of mountain run-off flows through this valley. There are plenty of stones in the river's streambed—stones both large and small. That gives it some structure. The river is running clear, too. A classic trout stream, this is one of the biggest, most attractive stretches of water I've ever seen in the Adirondacks. It also happens to be one of the few rivers in the continental United States that begins and ends in a wilderness area. Cold River's journey from the High Peaks to Long Lake is a short but glorious one. What a beauty! Just gazing upon it is reason enough to tramp the miles of muddy trail required to get here.

I'm bone tired but can't pass up an opportunity like this. Before firing up my stove and making dinner, I go back up to the shelter and get my fly rod. A single mayfly has peeled off a swirling, amber pool. That's all it takes to motivate me. So then, for the first time since West Canada Lake, I cast for trout. Nothing rises, but I enjoy the ritual of casting anyway. Tomorrow, when I'm more alert, I'll make a real effort to catch something. But for now, it's enough just getting my line wet.

Dinner is an expedient affair as it usually is at the end of a long hiking day. I hoist my food bag off the ground just after dusk, then settle into my sleeping bag for the night. I make a journal entry by headlamp light while listening to the soothing white noise of rushing water. A handful of jellybeans, chased by a cup of hot tea, seems a great luxury. The autumnal tints of the surrounding trees fade slowly to darkness. Times like this, when I'm warm and dry and relatively clean, with the forest all to myself, I feel just a tad guilty. What have I done to deserve this? Hauling a full pack all day doesn't seem like enough of a price to pay for such an exquisite moment. Seriously now. Why am I so lucky to be here?

A couple mosquitoes buzz around my head, making me wonder if perhaps I mailed the mosquito netting back home too soon. But a brisk evening breeze takes care of them. By candlelight I stare into the still forest until I hear an owl hooting way off in the distance. Then silence and fatigue finally overtake me. I blow out the candle and fade away. And the river courses through my dreams all night long.

MORNING EARLY. I'm tired, bug-bitten, and achy. While getting dressed, I sort through my clothes. The line between wet and dry has blurred to the point where this process now seems absurd. I have a clean, dry t-shirt and an unused pair of socks in a watertight bag. Aside from that, everything else feels a little damp in the chilly air. Everything, that is, except the socks I wore yesterday. They are downright wet. And my boots are even worse. I don't think they have completely dried out since I started this trip. I toss back a couple ibuprofen and stumble out of the shelter. My food bag is soaked. Must have rained overnight. Everything inside it is okay, though. Good thing.

Once again I pour a bag full of stale raisin bran into a bowl of reconstituted milk. That and a handful of trail mix is my breakfast. I take no pleasure in it. Twelve days on the trail, and I am beginning to miss the many small amenities of civilization. Thank heaven Lake Placid is only two and a half days away. Then again, I'm not enthusiastic about leaving the woods. Every backcountry excursion comes down to this, it seems. Deeply mixed feelings.

A half hour later, once I'm fully dressed and awake, my outlook on life is much better. The sun rises slowly over the misty stream while I sip a cup of hot coffee. Chickadees cheep serenely from the conifers. A ray of sunlight catches the orange and yellow leaves of maples and birches just right, and once again I feel like the luckiest man in the world. It's a good day for a hike. I relish the prospect of following Cold River for miles on end.

Is that wood smoke I smell? I shoulder my pack and leave camp in something of a rush. I half expect to find other backpackers tending a campfire somewhere up the trail. At lean-to #4, I find a torn and abandoned sleeping bag along with some other trash, but no indication that anyone actually stayed here last night. And the fire pit is stone cold. Still, I smell wood smoke…or is it something else? There are scores of dead cedars along the stream. I pull the bough of a dried-out cedar to my nose and, yes, I think that's it. I sniff the yellow underbrush along the trail that's soaking my pants. Then I sniff a fern that's half green and half brown. No, not wood smoke, but the forest itself at the end of the growing season. It's the dryleaf smell of autumn.

I amble slowly past a huge pool in the river called Big Eddy. The sun's reflection dances across rippling waters. A sudden blast of heat triggers a desire to strip off all my clothes and dive in. Is this the last desperate gasp of summer? The urge to submerge quickly passes as clouds obscure the sun. I sweat my way up a short, steep, brushy incline before easing back into the soothing shade of cedars.

Several blue jays sweep past me while I hike, protesting my intrusion. A hawk circles high over the river. Whitewater roars over and around smooth rocks nearby. Through the trees I spot several deep pools that must be holding trout. But I keep moving, daydreaming of a much earlier time when roaming Iroquois bands left their tracks along this stream. And for a moment I am a buckskinned woodsman straight out of a James Fenimore Cooper novel. But no, the trekking poles in hand remind me that I'm a twenty-first century backpacker, worlds away from any kind of frontier. Still I feel incredibly fortunate to be this deep in the wild. I celebrate, breath by heavy breath, the magnificence of the dark forest all around me, identifying more with those moccasin-wearing people of the past than with any of my cell-phone-toting contemporaries.

"In God's wildness lies the hope of the world," John Muir once wrote, "The great, fresh, unblighted, unredeemed wilderness." No doubt a proclamation of this sort seems ridiculous to those who never leave the developed lowlands, but out here it makes perfect sense. Wildness is "the hope of the world," yes, as if nothing else will do the trick. "Unredeemed wilderness," absolutely, as if to remind us that not all good things are manmade. I have known this for years. But the passage of time and the tedium of the daily routine take their toll on me as they do on all lovers of wild nature. Back in the lowlands, I forget what is real while sinking slowly into a quagmire of abstractions, nagging desires, and vague discontent. It takes something remarkable like this, Cold River, to snap out me of it.

LATE MORNING, I stop at Seward lean-to for a short rest. I drop my pack in the shelter then hobble down to the water to look around while refueling my body and slaking my thirst. Cascading whitewater carves a channel in a huge, sloping wall of rock. It looks something like the spillway of a dam. Here the river pours into a broad, deep pool that swirls around a bit before continuing downstream. My guidebook calls this Miller's Falls. It must be quite impressive in the spring. But right now its quieter, end-of-summer mood matches my own, so I kick back and enjoy a rather sedate display of rushing water. The waterfall is easy on the eyes, as are the trees framing the river.

Amber water and grey rock beneath a white sky, amid forest green, gold, crimson, and flaming orange—unspeakable beauty. No photograph could ever do it justice. I'd like to write a poem about this place, but I don't think that would do it justice, either. So instead I sit cross-legged in deep reverence, groping for words to flesh out a prayer. The words don't come but I pray all the same. And when finally I get up, abandoning the scene, I resolve to celebrate beauty more and brood about the human condition less. Then I shoulder my pack and move on.

I don't get very far up the trail before the alluring sights and sounds of Cold River finally get to me. I drop my pack at what could've been a campsite once, then break out my rod. And for the next hour or so, I'm a fly fisherman not a hiker.

I hop from one stone to another along the stream's rocky bank, plying roily waters for that sleek, aquatic creature. To my great delight, a trout rises to my fly once, twice, then a third time. Working the seam of fast-moving riffles over and over, I finally hook a feisty brook trout. I land him with little ceremony. The bright blue and orange spots on its flanks glisten in the sunlight as I hold the small, wriggling fish tentatively in my wet hands. Then I slip him back into the drink. I continue fishing even as a dark cloud rolls overhead and drops its load—just enough rain to make rock-hopping treacherous. I don't care. I keep casting as if this is what I was born to do, until the sun breaks through the clouds and it's reflection on the river dazzles me.

My fly snags on the cedars during a backcast. That's what it takes to shake me out of my joyous delirium. I snap off the leader then reel in my line. Enough's enough. I've got to get moving again, so I put away my rod and hoist the heavy pack to my shoulders. What time is it? Well past noon and I have miles to go before reaching Rondeau's place. Yeah, I've got to keep moving. Can't stay on this river forever. My wife will be waiting for me in Lake Placid on Sunday. That's the day after tomorrow. And Lake Placid is still twenty miles away.

An hour of hard hiking puts me across Ouluska Pass Brook and past the lean-to named after it. Then I'm following the remnants of an old woods road, wondering where the remains of Rondeau's hermitage are located. My guidebook isn't clear about this. Have I passed the side trail to it already? When the NPT leaves the old woods road and starts climbing a knoll, I become confused. Then all of a sudden I enter a small clearing in the woods, not ten yards wide, and there before me are two steel buckets hanging from a wooden sign nailed to a tree. The sign says:

RONDEAU

HERMIT OF COLD RIVER

1912–1950

I have arrived. I drop my pack, sit down, and break out my food bag. It's almost two o'clock.

Chapter 19

NOAH JOHN RONDEAU took up residence deep in the Adirondacks where few people ever go. Calling himself the Mayor of Cold River, he came to this remote corner of the woods early in the century and stayed here until the big storm of 1950 forced him out. He was friendly to whatever visitors came his way. He hunted, fished, and trapped. He was self-educated, loved to read, and kept a journal. The Conservation Department tolerated him for the most part, though he had more than one run-in with Fish and Game officials over hunting violations. He lived in a wooden hut on the knoll where I am now sitting quietly. A pile of rusty implements rests beneath the sign with his name on it—proof positive that his life out here was both hard and simple. I can only imagine what it must've been like.

He picked a good spot. This knoll is high enough above the river to dispel any concerns he might have had about spring flooding, yet far enough below the adjoining ridges to escape the worst of winter winds. The sky to the south is wide open so there was ample daylight here during the darkest months. He was close enough to the old woods road to use it regularly, yet far enough away from it to be missed by passers-by. Right in the middle of the river valley, this must have been a good place to catch deer on the move. Good fishing in nearby pools, as well. Yeah, I can see all the advantages of living here, but it takes a special kind of person to be alone in deep woods for extended periods of time. I couldn't do it. I enjoy being by myself for a week or two, but for years on end, well, that's another matter. Like all hermits, Rondeau must have been very comfortable with himself—comfortable to say the least. I finish my lunch in the phantom company of the old hermit, then move on.

The trail leaves Cold River just beyond Rondeau's place, linking back up with the old woods road, then climbing steadily into a particularly quiet stretch of forest. I pass a couple beaver ponds barely visible through the trees. The occasional woodpecker knocks in the distance. Otherwise it's just me, myself, and the woods. This section of the NPT seems rather lackluster after such an interesting walk along the river. I use my trekking poles to avoid the worst mud holes and balance myself while negotiating downed trees. Aside from that, I'm on autopilot, tramping from trail marker to trail marker. Long distance hiking usually comes to this.

WHILE PLODDING ALONG, I ponder the many uses and abuses of wild country. I recall reading a statement made in an ADK publication called *With Wilderness at Heart*: "A major problem of Conservation is to know just where the saturation point is." In other words, how much impact is too much? The Adirondack Mountain Club promotes backcountry recreation, but the more they succeed, the more places like this take a beating. How many people can enjoy a wilderness before it ceases being a wilderness? Right now I have this country all to myself, but that's not the norm. In the middle of summer, these woods are full of people. Wild places can't stay wild for long with a constant stream of hikers flowing through them. On the other hand, they can't exist for just a handful of people like me. That's bad economics and even worse politics. So they have to be *somewhat* accessible. A balance must be struck, no doubt, between preserving the wild and people enjoying it.

On a larger scale, a balance must be struck between the preservation and development of the Adirondacks as a whole. A thousand new buildings pop up every year inside the Blue Line. Traffic on the roads is steadily increasing over time. Listen to those who live and work in the Adirondacks year round and you'll get an earful of mixed messages. Most of them want to see greater economic opportunity in the towns and villages that they call home, yet few want their beloved mountains co-opted by the rich folks flocking here from the big cities. It's a conundrum to be sure.

On the grand scale, the planet itself is in danger of being overdeveloped. There were only a billion and a half people living on Earth a hundred years ago. Today there are over six billion of us and our numbers are still growing. Add to this the simple fact that every year millions more people in developing countries become big, middle-class consumers, thus stressing global resources even more, and the long term prospects for wilderness preservation look grim. Certainly those who measure the quality of their lives by dollars alone see unrestricted growth as a good thing. But to those of us who think wild places have intrinsic value, this growth poses a great threat.

So what do we do? We support various non-profit organizations dedicated to preserving as much of the wild as possible, even if it comes at the expense of economic development. As Roderick Nash said in his book, *Wilderness and the American Mind*, "Wildland will remain wild only as a result of deliberate human choice." But he also pointed out that the appreciation of wild nature is a "full stomach phenomenon," practiced mostly by rich, educated, urbanites. While saving the rain forest may appeal to those of us living in relative luxury thousands of miles away, it's a hard sell to Brazilian peasants who just want to feed their families.

The preservation of the wild is often portrayed as an all-or-nothing struggle between businesspeople and environmentalists, with both sides having simple, clearly defined objectives. But there's more to it than that. Much more. Ultimately, it's a longstanding argument about how we choose to live our lives—"we" being each and every one of us on the planet. It's about what we value, how much we value it, and the relationship of that value to sheer economic necessity. These are fundamental matters, certainly, reaching far beyond the pleasure of a walk through deep woods or making a fast buck. Quick answers to problems of this magnitude are as superficial as the people advocating them. Real solutions demand profound changes regarding how we perceive our selves and the world. And changes of this sort don't come easy.

How much wilderness is enough wilderness? During moments like these, deep in the forest and totally self-absorbed, I am inclined to say the more the better. And most of my nature-loving friends would agree. But to the majority of poor people on the planet, vast stretches of undeveloped land seem a luxury they can ill afford. And yet they need it. Whether they realize it or not, they can't be fully human in the complete absence of the wild any more than I can. After all, the wild is within us. It is as much a part of what we are as tool-making, language, and abstract ideas.

THE HIKE PAST MOUNTAIN POND is disappointing. There are so many conifers in the way that I can't get a good look at the water. Not that it matters. I've seen plenty of ponds on this trip, so seeing or not seeing this one isn't going to make a great deal of difference to me. Besides, the only body of water I really care about right now is Duck Hole, and that's still a couple miles away. Upon reaching an improved woods road, I pull out my map. My guidebook calls this road the Ward Brook Truck Trail. It goes directly to my home for the night.

The trail to Duck Hole is easy to follow. I pass a middle-aged couple settling into a lean-to for the evening but don't stop to chat with them. I just nod their way and keep moving. A few minutes later, I hear the sound of rushing water. Then a bridge suddenly appears. After crossing the bridge, I slip down to the edge of Moose Creek to refill my water bottles. I rest, rehydrate, and fuel up with an energy bar before finishing my walk.

Duck Hole looks like the Promised Land as it emerges from the forest. Its placid water, surrounded by mountains, mirrors a vast expanse of overcast sky. I enjoy the view while meandering across an open field to an empty lean-to. Upon reaching the shelter, I spot another one a hundred yards away, right next to the pond's outlet stream. Much easier access to water over there, so I walk over and claim that shelter instead. Then it occurs to me that no one is camped at this pond. How odd. Duck Hole is one of those places visited by hundreds of backpackers every year, and tonight's Friday night. I figured it would be crawling with people. I expected both shelters to be full and a small village of tents set up nearby, as well. But here I am by myself. Just me and a lone beaver swimming in broad circles around the pond.

A drizzle commences while I'm unpacking my things. Talk about good luck! I landed here just in time. Not that that makes any difference. A light rain dampened the forest this morning, so I've been wet and muddy all day. I've also been sweating constantly. I probably smell bad enough to offend that beaver over there. While pulling clothes and gear out of my pack, I clutter the lean-to floor. It isn't a pretty sight. One good look at the mess then I break into hysterical laughter. This trek of mine has turned into a real grunge fest. Almost all of my gear is wet and dirty, and something stinks to high heaven. I think it's the pair of socks I wore two days ago. They still haven't dried out. Or maybe it's my favorite brown t-shirt, worn too much this trip. It's beyond redemption. I'm sure my wife will make me throw it away when I get home. I string a couple lines inside the shelter, then hang up everything to dry.

Down by the pond's outlet, I notice the heavy flow of water over a wooden dam. Is this normal? I also notice that the footbridge shown in my guidebook is missing. It must have washed away. Good thing I'm not hiking south tomorrow. The outlet stream looks easy enough to wade across, but I wouldn't want to start a day's hike that way. I ponder this while trying to imagine how much work it'll take to replace that bridge. Yet another project for the DEC and the Adirondack Mountain Club. And the list keeps growing.

Dusk. I fire up my stove and eat dinner by twilight. It's almost dark by the time I sling my food bag in the trees. A few fish rise along the pond's wandering shoreline, but it's too late to do anything about it. The bats are out already. Maybe I'll do a little fishing tomorrow morning before heading north. Or maybe not. Depends on the weather and how I feel when I get out of bed. I switch into nearly dry camp clothes before retiring to my sleeping bag with a cup of lukewarm tea and the last remaining handful of jellybeans. Bats swoop through the diminishing light, the beaver swims back and forth across the pond, and all is calm. When the rain ends, the pond becomes glass. An owl hoots in the distance.

By headlamp I study my guidebook and maps. I'm a little concerned about the drowned lands to the north, between Duck Hole and Moose Pond. Limps-a-Little warned me about it, as did that other thru-hiker I ran into yesterday morning. The trail is flooded in several places, thanks to beavers. Could be a challenge getting through there, especially with all the rain that has fallen lately. It's only a twelve-mile hike out of these woods, but that could take more than a day if I'm detouring around a bunch of beaver ponds. No matter. Judy isn't expecting me in Lake Placid until Sunday afternoon, so I have plenty of time. Still, I hope I don't get bogged down. I'm not in the mood for it.

Chapter 20

ALITTLE PAST MIDNIGHT, I heed Nature's call. No, not the call of the wild, nor a call to arms in her defense, but that simple, watery urge down below that every camper dreads in the middle of the night. I really shouldn't drink tea right before going to bed. Too late now. I crawl from my warm sleeping bag, cursing the Creator for designing me this way. I slip on a pair of flip flops that I keep on hand specifically for moments like this, then venture out of the shelter and into the cool, damp night.

I gaze into the all-consuming darkness while doing my business. The night sky is wide open. There's not a cloud in sight, and the stars seem close enough to touch. Lots and lots of stars—a show one can only enjoy in a place like this, far away from city lights. "Voluptuous presences," the naturalist and stargazer Chet Raymo calls them in his book, *Honey From Stone*. While standing slack-jawed before them in deep forest silence, I have to agree with him that "stars are more than we bargained for." Indeed. Their luminescent reality seems to undercut my own. In a universe so vast, how can my earthly existence be anything but a dream?

I turn slowly while taking it all in. There's the stellar "W" of Cassiopeia and the huge cross of Cygnus in the Milky Way. There's the Great Square of Pegasus directly overhead and just the hint of Andromeda, the spiral galaxy nearby that's so much like ours. The Pleiades, that familiar cluster of stars, seems closer and brighter than usual for some reason, as does the V-shaped star formation in the middle of Taurus. It's all so amazing—a cosmic drama playing out before me, cold and distant yet strangely beautiful.

I contemplate the immensity of it all while staring deep into space, recalling random bits of astronomical knowledge I've picked up over the years. I recall how big some of those stars are—the biggest ones, like Betelgeuse, being four hundred times larger than our Sun. I recall that some of those stars aren't really stars at all but great clouds of gas like Orion Nebula. I remember reading that there are over a hundred billion galaxies in the universe. That comes to twenty million galaxies for every star I can see. No, that can't be right. It can't possibly be that many. I don't have enough grey matter between the ears to grasp Nature on such a grand scale, so I let it go. I've got to get back to bed, anyway. Big hiking day tomorrow.

DAYBREAK. Duck Hole is obscured by fog. I putter about camp, finishing breakfast while slowly packing up. I'm eager to get back on the trail, but it takes another cup of strong coffee to spur me to action. I pop two ibuprofen tablets, patch my feet, and stretch out my knotted muscles the best I can. I convince myself that I'm doing well for a fifty-year-old who's been on the trail for two weeks, then shoulder my pack and go. I can feel the sun's warmth on my skin while crossing the clearing. It won't be long before the fog burns off. When it does the sun will shine brightly, I'm sure.

Up the trail I go, hugging Roaring Brook. The stream glistens in the early morning sunlight. I break through dozens of brand new spiders' webs while pressing forward. Then a set of large deer tracks appears beneath my feet and the silk vanishes. Suddenly it occurs to me that other animals might be using this trail, as well. I study the ground and soon spot another set of tracks, larger and more like a predator's. Recent rain has softened the muddy trail so the tracks are deep and well defined. Those are bear tracks, no doubt. And when the deer tracks leave the trail, there's still no spider's silk. That can mean only one thing. A black bear must be in front of me, not too far ahead. Suddenly there's a real chance of seeing that elusive creature. This sharpens my senses as I venture deeper into wild country.

The trail twists and turns around boulders and downed trees. It narrows considerably while climbing into a tight mountain pass. I step lightly, panting quietly while placing the tips of my trekking poles between roots and rocks. I sweat heavily during the humid ascent. The underbrush soaks my pants. I slip in the mud once, catching myself, then slip again and fall to my knees. I stifle a grunt while getting back to my feet. The bear is close—I just know it—and I don't want to spook him. I want a glimpse of that creature, however brief it might be. I'm deep in the woods and longing to make contact with a like-minded other. Both bear and I have sought refuge in this shady forest.

When I enter the notch, the big tracks leave the trail. I look around but there's no bear in sight. All the same, I sense its presence here. Maybe the bear is long gone; maybe he's watching me. *Someone* is watching me— that's for certain. The forest has eyes. Beneath clubmoss, beetles look on. Red efts and toads take note as I walk by. A thrush sounds alarm. The very rocks and trees register my footsteps. A mist swirls around me. Then it happens: a sudden surge of emotion erupting from somewhere deep within. I let out a gut-busting howl of delight, exhilarated by a profound sense of connectedness. All things are woven together in this wild world, including me. I stop just beyond the height of land to catch my breath. I drop my pack and wipe sweat from my face. Then I smile broadly while basking in the green infinity.

This terribly wild place is *my* country—mine in a way that mocks all simplistic notions of ownership. This country is mine because it possesses me. The wild has just reached deep inside and seized the very core of my being. Now it won't let go. It's been a long time since I last felt this way. I'm crazy with it—crazy with forest joy. I can't get enough of it. I love being out here. I love the damp, mossy, fecund glory of it all. I love this primal immediacy, the rampant assertion of life everywhere I look, the woody chaos. Cold-blooded logic carries little weight here. The wild reality all around me is clearly beyond anything I can fully, rationally comprehend. But I don't care. I revel in it. I chug down half a liter of water then howl again as water dribbles off my chin. Just being here is reason enough to inhale deeply, then exhale with all the force I can muster, as if blowing out all the bad faith of the lowlands.

I can't help but sing as I meander down the trail sloping north out of the notch. My boisterous singing diminishes to a low hum, though, as I consider the possibility of spotting some rare forest creature—a fisher cat or pine marten, maybe. But it's a glorious day so I hum away. I'm following a trail winding through the trees while beams of sunlight illuminate moosewood leaves, bracken, and ferns. I hum in cadence with trekking poles clicking against roots and rocks. Then I run into water, lots of it, while dropping down fast into the Moose Creek drainage basin.

Beaver ponds crop up everywhere. Some of them have been here a while; others are under construction. A set of hunter's ribbons guides me around one such pond. I cross the dam of another as if crossing a balance beam. The blue NPT markers aren't much help getting through here. Some of them cling to trees in the middle of ponds. Others have disappeared. Those bucktoothed engineers have created a formidable obstacle course.

I take a straight, well-honed stick from a brand new dam and break off the weak end of it. Then I use the saw blade of my Swiss Army knife to clean up the thicker end. And there it is: one sturdy walking stick, compliments of Mr. Beaver. Thank you very much. I strap the trekking poles to my pack and set forth with a brand new pilgrim's staff firmly in hand. This stick better suits my frame of mind right now—now that the wild has consumed me. It's inexplicable, really, this sudden change of heart. It's as if nothing in the whole world could be more important than being right here right now, knee-deep in beaver pond muck. Have I gone mad? What's the matter with me? Nothing, absolutely nothing. I've come home, that's all.

I cross the stream once, then cross it again. Moose Pond can't be far away. And when I catch a glimpse of it through the trees, I realize that I've just walked the entire Northville-Placid Trail. That is, between this hike and another one many years ago, I've hiked every foot of it both north and south of here. I start recognizing the terrain as the trail climbs steadily uphill. Then suddenly the Moose Pond lean-to appears. I drop my pack while looking around in utter amazement. This place is impossibly familiar. How long has it been since Judy and I camped here? Seven years ago? Eight? I've passed through some kind of time warp. It seems like I was here just a few weeks ago. But I remember being able to see the pond from this shelter, and now a wall of young trees blocks the view.

While sitting on the edge of the lean-to, I recall that outing back in '98: how hard it rained that afternoon, the mist rising from the pond afterward, and our first glimpse of the Sawtooth Range in the distance. We cooked and ate spaghetti on this very spot. A silver-haired fellow and his fifteen-year-old granddaughter came along the next day. They ate lunch here before continuing south. I imagine my eldest granddaughter and I doing the same thing someday. This rattles me. I am overwhelmed by the familiarity of this place, by the stark beauty of the wild country through which I just passed, and the inexorable creep of time. It's too much, too much! So then, without warning, I break into tears.

Time is relative. Right now I feel like I'm fifty going on thirty. Young at heart, old in years. But not that old. I probably have many years ahead of me. Or I could die tomorrow. If that happens, at least I'll be able to say that I've lived a full life. I've been more fortunate than most. My bless-ings are many: a loving spouse, children, and grandchildren, good health, meaningful work, regular access to wild country—I stop counting my blessings at this. There's no reason to continue. Spending time alone in deep woods is the luckiest break of all. For decades I've been coming out here, strengthening my connection to the earth in ways that wouldn't have been possible back in Ohio where I grew up. And to think that I almost killed myself when I was a teenager. What a waste that would've been! I would have missed all this. But that didn't happen, so here I am, thirty-five years later and still breathing, still going strong. Here I am with only a hazy recollection of the driving forces behind all that teen angst. Time changes everything. Now I'm an over-the-hill hiker grooving on the wild. Yeah, I've been lucky, incredibly lucky.

THE TRAIL BEYOND MOOSE POND rises steadily into a narrow notch between Three Peaks and Street Mountain. I climb it slowly. With beaver stick in hand, I am now more of a woodswalker than a thru-hiker. No rush. I watch the tiny rivulets of water switch direction in the notch—flowing south towards the Moose Creek at first, then north towards Chubb River. When the trail descends, I check my map to verify that it's downhill all the way from here to Averyville Road where the NPT ends. I'll have to stop and make camp soon. Either that or leave the trail early. This is some-thing I hadn't even considered until now.

Just below the notch, I come to a trail junction. Wanika Falls is only ten minutes away. Not even that. I remember how impressive those falls looked back in '98, after the big storm. That'll be a good place to stop for lunch, so I follow the side trail towards the sound of cascading water. I reach the falls much faster than expected.

Wanika Falls drops from a greater height than I remember. I forgot about its upper tier. Not much water coming down, though—just a trickle compared to '98. There's blue sky directly overhead and blinding sunlight glancing off tumbling water. A large, deep pool ripples at the base of the falls. I drop my pack and hobble down to the water's edge. Before filling my bottles, I splash cold water on my face, washing away the morning's sweat. Lunch is an unhurried affair. I nestle in the rocks and daydream about my last visit here while munching away, occasionally staring up at the falls. The steady roar of water keeps deep thoughts at bay. That's fine by me. I'm happy enough just being here.

After lunch, I mobilize at a snail's pace. The tenor of this outing has just changed. Now it's not so much about finishing this hike as it is staying in the woods as long as possible. I'm tired, dirty, and sick of being wet, but I don't want to rush out of here. So I amble back to the main trail, then creep northward as slowly as possible, admiring the rugged landscape along the way.

The headwaters of the Chubb River roar through a small gorge, rushing from Wanika Falls to marshy flats a few miles away. The forest gradually brightens as conifers give way to broadleaf trees. Two backpackers, a man and a woman in their early twenties, appear just as I'm crossing a high, narrow footbridge spanning the stream. They are the first people I've seen since passing that lean-to couple yesterday. They are on their way to Wanika Falls, where they intend to spend the night—just the two of them. Good thing I didn't make camp there.

I daydream through a forest awash in autumnal color. I wade through dried leaves—crimson, orange, gold, and fading green. Still plenty of mud holes to negotiate, but who cares? I'm drifting downhill, intoxicated by the smell of a forest that has moved well beyond summer. Yet another blessing, this delightful stretch of trail. And the sun, absent for days on end, keeps me company for the rest of the afternoon.

Chapter 21

NORTH OF WANIKA FALLS, the trail is so easy to hike that I cover two miles of it in one dreamy hour. And when finally I snap out of my late afternoon reverie, it occurs to me that I've just overshot the two best places to draw water and make camp. How stupid of me. Feeder streams are scarce in these parts. Now I'm forced to keep hiking until I reach Snow Brook—the last dependable water source this side of Averyville Road. My pack grows heavy as I follow a crease in the land that holds a tiny rivulet. I'm tempted to make camp here, but no, Snow Brook must be just ahead, so I keep going. Shortly after the trail flattens out, it crosses a swell in a stream where beavers have been hard at work. Is this Snow Brook? I'm not sure. It doesn't matter. The water's too brackish, so I keep going.

Now the trail's a muddy mess and I'm not happy about it. I stop a middle-aged hiker heading south towards some trail-less summit and ask him if he has passed any feeder streams. When he says no, I start cursing. He must think I'm a real jerk. I wish him a good day with all the pleasantness I can muster, then continue cursing down the trail. I'm mad at my guidebook and outdated maps. I'm mad at myself. I've already hiked several miles farther than I intended to go today and still don't have a water source. It's getting late. If I'm not careful, I'll end up leaving these woods this evening.

Bogged down, slipping around in the mud so much that I can feel blisters developing on the *side* of my feet, I curse even more. Then the trail rises slowly towards Heaven Hill. I can't be more than two miles from Averyville Road. I've got to stop. I drop my pack as soon as the trail crests the hill's western shoulder. I tramp around in circles a few dozen yards off trail until finally I find a relatively flat, dry spot to pitch my tarp. This'll have to do. I don't want to camp without a water source, but it's either that or finish the NPT tonight.

Everything is harder when you're tired. It takes a half hour to set up the tarp and twice as long to sling a line in the trees for my food bag. I pull back a mat of forest duff and fashion a small fire pit on the exposed earth. My campfire won't be more than a foot across, but that's big enough. I string a line between two trees and drape the wettest, dirtiest clothes over it. Gathering wood is easy. I have an armload in ten minutes. And there it is: home sweet home. The nice thing about backpacking is that you can make camp anywhere, water source notwithstanding. This isn't the best camp in the world, but it'll do.

THE SMALL FIRE BURNING IN FRONT OF ME illuminates the darkness. I feed thumb-sized sticks into it one at a time. The ribbon of smoke curling from the campfire keeps the mosquitoes at bay. Burning embers give my eyes something to focus on. I marvel at the fact that I've nearly finished hiking the Northville-Placid Trail. It's Saturday night. I've been in the woods for two weeks. I hear dogs barking in the distance and cars motoring along Averyville Road not far away. These are the first sounds of civilization I've heard since leaving Long Lake three days ago. I am both comforted and saddened by it.

After catching a whiff of the clothes hanging from the nearby line, I start giggling like a homeless man enjoying a private joke. No doubt about it, this has been a grungy outing. Won't need a headlamp when I go off to pee in the darkness. I'll be able to find my way back to camp by the smell of it. How long has it been since I last took a dip in a lake? Don't even want to think about how dirty I am. And my clothes, well, some of them are absolutely disgusting. At least one article of clothing is a biohazard. But I still have that clean t-shirt and pair of socks under plastic. I'm saving those for tomorrow. I'll put them on right before going into town.

Dinner is an energy bar and a handful of trail mix. Don't want to waste precious water cleaning up. I take two good swigs from one water bottle, thus emptying it. The other is two-thirds full. I'll save that for morning. How ironic is this, to spend so much time in and around water only to have my last camp be a dry one. But that's the way things go sometimes. I'm just glad that I didn't hike out of the woods tonight. I would have felt cheated.

The small fire goes out by itself. I stir the embers into oblivion then slip beneath the tarp. I'm exhausted. I'm so tired I could sleep anywhere. But my bed is quite comfortable, oddly enough. I've pitched my tarp over a patch of humus several inches thick. Wood frogs peep from nearby wetlands. They're noisy but they won't keep me awake. Could be difficult getting to sleep, though, with all my aches and pains. I down a pair of ibuprofen with a little water. Once that kicks in, I drift effortlessly into the land of dreams.

DAYBREAK COMES QUICKLY. I'm up and moving about as the first rays of sunlight filter through the trees on Heaven Hill. With only a half liter of water left, I forego the luxury of coffee. I use a few ounces of water to brush my teeth after breakfast, though. There's a limit to how much grunge a guy can take. I pop a couple more ibuprofen then start breaking camp. I flick slugs off my clothes before packing them away. I put on the last clean t-shirt, saving the pair of clean socks for later. Once my boots are laced up, the dampness that I feel from the waist down isn't so bad. Grunge or no, I'm in pretty good spirits this morning. I slept well last night and it looks like it's going to be another beautiful day in the woods.

The forest is all green and gold now. I savor it while ambling along the trail. There's a touch of brown in the understory, reminding me that the growing season is over. Although my newfound walking stick is wooden, it clicks loudly against the rocks. No matter. I don't expect to see any wildlife this morning. But the forest itself is a pleasant sight, now that it's mostly hardwoods with just enough conifers to make it interesting. Why do I love the woods so much? Hard to say. It's just a bunch of trees. But trees do something for me that open spaces do not.

Do my eyes deceive me? Less than half a mile down the trail I come to a trickle of water narrow enough to step across. I look to my right and see a jumble of moss-covered rocks in a deep-cut ravine. A spring! What a godsend! I splash the cold, clear water on my face, then break out my pump. I drink as much water as my stomach can hold before filling my bottles.

Not too far beyond the spring, I come upon another big surprise. The trail drops to a pool just above a brand new beaver dam. Not a big pool, but big enough to effectively to block my path. With tightly packed spruces on either side of the trail, I have no choice but to traverse the submerged puncheon spanning the pool. I do this with great reluctance, steadying myself with my walking stick. What a relief to reach the other side! Why didn't one of those southbound hikers warn me about this? Call it a parting shot from the beavers. Less than a mile from trail's end, they're making sure I won't forget them. After scrambling to higher ground, I bid farewell to my bucktoothed companions. We'll meet again, I'm sure. But not today.

The long stretch of flat trail following the Chubb River looks quite familiar. I remember it well from my scouting trip this summer. The end is near. Sure enough, I pass a trail register and pop out of the woods. And it's over just like that. I stumble across the nearly empty parking lot, dropping my pack next to the Chubb River. A car turns into the parking lot and two young hikers step out. I ignore them while washing the worst of the mud from my boots and pants. Clouds drift overhead, but they aren't threatening. It's a cool, dry, partly cloudy day. The three-mile walk into Lake Placid this morning will be easy. All I have to do is rest up a little before finishing my hike.

Chapter 22

FROM THE TRAILHEAD PARKING LOT, the asphalt road into Lake Placid rises for a quarter mile. I keep to its gravel shoulder, walking stick in hand, garnering stares from people passing in cars and trucks. A little over a mile down the road, I reach an intersection. I take a short break beneath a sign marking the northernmost terminus of the Northville-Placid Trail. The sign seems rather out of place, being as far as it is from the actual trailhead. I patch my feet one last time, then put on the precious pair of clean, dry socks. Yessir, I'm going to town in style.

Beyond the trail sign and across the busy intersection, the landscape is urban. I amble past a long row of houses. I nod, say hello to a couple tourists standing in front of a train museum, then quickly break eye contact. I try to force a smile but it doesn't come. Not sure why. The transition from forest to countryside to townscape is too abrupt, I guess. The change hits especially hard while I'm walking along Route 73 into the heart of Lake Placid. I feel awkward and out of place lumbering up the sidewalk with a huge pack on my back. But this is silly. Hikers are a common sight in the Adirondacks, aren't they?

Late morning. I drop my pack next to a plastic trash can before stepping inside a convenience store. I pour myself a cup of coffee, take a cookie from a small display, and grab a bottle of apple juice from the cooler. I get into line at the checkout, telling myself that I'm just another customer. Be cool. After a quick exchange of money and pleasantries with the clerk behind the counter, I go back outside. Once I'm finished eating and drinking in the parking lot, I stuff the half-full bottle of apple juice in my pack and slip around the back to pee in the bushes. Can't face a public restroom just yet. So I do my business, then shoulder the pack and continue trekking deeper into the city.

Downtown Lake Placid is bustling with tourists. This should come as no surprise to me. It's a warm, partly sunny Sunday in early autumn. Church bells ring as I settle into an Adirondack chair in a small park in the middle of town. High noon. The park faces Mirror Lake. The lake is as serene as the people around me. I take a swig from the apple juice bottle while enjoying the play of sunlight between clouds. I kick off my boots after making sure that no one is within smelling distance. A short while later, I put them back on so that I can go into a nearby restaurant and purchase a slice of pizza. The pizza is hot, fresh, and greasy. I relish each bite while lounging in the park.

Judy catches up to me a short while later. The pizza I just ate confounds her lunch plans, so we go for beer after stashing my backpack in the trunk of her car. While sitting at a shaded table on the terrace of a small restaurant, we catch up. The conversation is pleasant enough, but what isn't said hangs heavy between us. No need to voice it, really. We've been here before. Judy is very much in the swing of things while I'm still somewhere in the wilderness. We both know that time will correct this dissonance. Just have to be patient, that's all.

Shortly after we check into the hotel room that Judy has reserved, I take a hot shower. In terms of sheer pleasure, this is hard to beat. When Judy asks if I'm up for a little window shopping, I say: "Sure, why not?" Better than hiding in a hotel room for the rest of the day. She has brought me a set of clean street clothes from home. I put them on, then we wander about town. Judy moves in and out of stores, making a few small purchases. I stay on the sidewalk for the most part, marveling at the gentility of this town and its inhabitants. Everyone seems so…sedate. I try to follow suit, speaking in soft tones while suppressing any natural impulses that might embarrass my wife.

By the time we go to dinner, I'm in a very strange frame of mind. The wine is excellent, the meal superb, and I'm thoroughly enjoying Judy's company. But there's a part of me that wants to hightail back to the forest, screaming all the way. It'll be months before I get another good fix of deep woods solitude—maybe years—and I'm already missing Cold River and West Canada Lake. But there's something disingenuous about this feeling. I could never live as Noah John Rondeau and French Louie did. I love my wife, family, and friends too much, not to mention the easy life here in the lowlands. Give it time, I tell myself. Civility will come back to me.

"HE WHO HAS ONCE EXPERIENCED the fascination of the woods-life never escapes its enticement," Charles Dudley Warner wrote in the 1880s, in his book about the Adirondacks called *In the Wilderness*. "In the memory nothing remains but its charm." How true that is—how painfully true. It's easy to romanticize the wild as Emerson, Thoreau, and others have. The word "sublime" comes quickly to a woodswalker's lips, even today. After a week or two in the forest, grooving with wild animals and dealing with the elements, I tune into a primal reality. But this passes with time, sadly, as I go about my business in the lowlands. So I keep going back to the woods. Memory is not enough. Eventually those of us enamored by the wild must return to it or go mad. Modern life, with all its abstractions and distractions, slowly unhinges us.

Smarter, wiser people have spoken more eloquently about the value of wilderness than I ever could. And there are those who fight for its preservation with a fervor that escapes me, I must confess. But this much I can say without reservation: Without access to wild country, a vital part of me would perish. I need it as much as I need food and water. Others feel the same way, I know. Yet there are those who think humankind would be better off if all things wild were firmly under our control—subdued, micromanaged, or eliminated altogether. The world would be one great big amusement park if they had their way. So I thank God for the Adirondacks and places like it, hoping that they'll still exist a thousand years from now, giving future generations a chance to experience what can only be experienced off the grid, deep in the forest. There is, after all, no substitute for wildness.